Wicked
Bisbee

Francine Powers

THE
History
PRESS

Published by The History Press
Charleston, SC
www.historypress.com

Front cover, clockwise from top left: author's collection; courtesy Bisbee Mining & Historical Museum, Opie Burgess Collection; photo attributed to E.J. Bellocq, Wikimedia Commons; author's collection; author's collection; *bottom background*: author's collection.
Back cover, bottom: author's collection.

First published 2023

Manufactured in the United States

ISBN 9781467154956

Library of Congress Control Number: 2023938571

For my children Brittany, Randy, Gigi and my grandson Andre.
Keep this book as a reminder that we must know the past, so we never repeat it.

CONTENTS

PREFACE

Having grown up in such a small town as Bisbee, Arizona, I have a lifetime of memories that have shaped my thoughts and impression of it as a serene and happy place. The old mining town has been the home of my family for generations, and I gladly took this opportunity to write about its history. I was surprised, while taking the "wicked" point of view, to discover a side of Bisbee I've never seen before. Although I've been collecting Bisbee history since I was a high school student and spent many years intensely studying its past, this darker take has shown me that it's important to chronicle all of a town's history, both the good and the bad.

Through the events I researched, uncovered and exposed, you will get a better understanding of how Bisbee has always had a place in the Wild West of American history.

INTRODUCTION

*I*f you get a chance to drive through the Bisbee Mule Pass Tunnel, located in the Mule Mountains of southeastern Arizona, you might feel as though you were traveling back in time. As soon as you exit the tunnel, the mood seems to glide into a different realm. It's extraordinary. Once hailed as the "Queen of Copper Camps" for its mining industry, Bisbee is now acknowledged as an artist's community. The underground operation stopped in 1974, and surface mining ended in 1975.

Originally, this area was in Pima County and was called the Southern Dragoon Mountains. In 1877, deep into these same peaks, U.S. Army lieutenant John A. Rucker with fifteen men of Company C, Sixth Cavalry, from Fort Bowie, along with John "Jack" Dunn, arrived. They were on an expedition to see if members of the Chiricahua Apache tribe had an encampment there. After Lieutenant Rucker and his group camped overnight, Dunn went on a mission to find good drinking water. He discovered a fresh spring flowing at Castle Rock and found an indication of the presence of lead, copper, silver and gold. Soon after, Rucker, Dunn and their packer, T.D. Byrne, claimed the first mine there and called it the Rucker. A few weeks later, a prospector with a long life of trauma and drama named Gorge Warren was grubstaked by Dunn to find more rich spots in the area. Warren was supposed to name Dunn in all notices of places he might find. Warren found more claims but never listed Dunn on any of the several he located.

Bisbee Mule Pass Tunnel, built in 1958. When you drive through it, you may be overcome with the sensation of floating back in time. *Courtesy Randy S. Powers.*

Only fifty-six days after the Rucker Mine was discovered, Warren found a second mining claim in the area, naming it the Mercy Mine. He is considered by some to be the "Father of Bisbee."

The mines and surrounding properties were solely owned in later years by the Phelps Dodge Company but are now owned by Freeport McMoRan Copper and Gold. The name of the town was given in honor of Judge

Bisbee, Arizona, circa 1935. *Author's collection.*

DeWitt Bisbee of the mining firm of Williams and Bisbee of San Francisco. He loaned $20,000 to the engineering firm Martin and Ballard to buy the Copper Queen prospect.

The Calumet & Arizona Mining Company decided that the nationally acclaimed City Beautiful movement would be an excellent model for the new townsite of Warren. It was completed around 1907. Other notable areas that sprang up in later Bisbee history include San Jose, Bakerville, Briggs, Don Luis, Galena, Tintown and Saginaw.

Bisbee has evolved over the decades, and there was a time when prostitutes were part of business culture and were allowed to work and live in the designated red-light district. Other groups were also designated from the rest of the town. Some of the schools and churches were segregated, and persons such as Mexican nationals and Mexican Americans were not allowed to work underground but only as surface laborers. The Hispanics and Yaqui Indians had to live in certain neighborhoods, such as Zacatecas Canyon, Chihuahua Hill and Tin-Town. In 1910, a petition was presented to the Bisbee City Council for a building for students of African descent to be constructed on the site of the pioneer cemetery. The property was at that time being sought after by the Warren District Commercial Club to make the old graveyard into a city park, which it is today.

In the early 1880s, widows of men killed in the mines and who were mostly of Irish decent decided to make a living by starting a laundry business. A group of Chinese people set up their own laundry operation at the same time, and because they were cheaper and more efficient, the widows were put out of business. There was much controversy and protesting by Bisbee miners, who said it was wrong what the Chinese businesses were doing to the widows. It was said that the Chinese workers were depriving the widows of the means of supporting their own families. There was an unwritten rule that prohibited "Orientals" from staying in Bisbee after sundown. They were allowed to come into the mining camp to sell fresh vegetables but had to leave before sundown.

Some Chinese people were known to defy the rule. A group decided to camp overnight at Castle Rock to get an early start on the next day's laundry orders. When they left the camp, some miners decided it was a good idea to dress a homemade dummy in the style of clothing the Chinese people wore and hang it from the limb of a tree near where the group was camping. On their return, a hired man sitting in a wagon pulled by horses cracked his whip and drove away. The dummy was left hanging from the limb of the tree. The members of the Chinese group were so frightened that they ran to the very top of the divide, approximately four miles away. After that, the laundry services owned by the widows became utterly successful.

Men from around the world were swarming into Bisbee for work in the late 1800s and early 1900s. There was a group of men from Cornwall, England. Generations of these men had worked as hard-rock miners and were experts at using dynamite. They were sturdy men built for such an undertaking. They were also excellent at being safe underground and being efficient. They were considered fantastic prospectors. These men were called "Cousin Jacks." The Cornish miners traveled the world, from Central and South America and Alaska to India and the United States of America. They played a large role in the formation of the Bisbee mines.

With the increase in population and mining success came some dissatisfactory situations, such as the thick smoke coming from the flumes of the copper smelter, located almost in the heart of the city. Because of the many restaurants, saloons, markets, hotels and houses placed in every nook and cranny of the narrow canyons, tons of garbage and raw sewage were dumped in some streets. The stench of the open sewage pits and the trash was horrendous. Owners of restaurants even threw carcasses of butchered

Early Castle Rock. Donkeys loaded with firewood. *Author's collection*.

Loading ore sacks onto the burros in Cochise County, late 1880s. *Author's collection*.

Lavender Pit, 1972. *Author's collection.*

animals into the alleys, where they decomposed, adding to the poor living conditions. These circumstances caused millions of flies to populate the area, triggering a great deal of health issues. Bisbee also had to contend with extreme flash floods from the monsoon rains and several devastating fires.

Despite these problems, the mines were producing about one million pounds of ore a month and had to transport one hundred tons a day by an eighteen-mule team to the town of Fairbank, which had the nearest train station, then on to Benson. Production was so good that the mining companies could afford to transport the ore to a smelter in Phoenixville, Pennsylvania.

At first, the mule teams went around the San Pedro Valley to get to Fairbank. P.H. Banning's place was a watering stop for the mules and drivers. Banning suggested that a road be built over the Mule Mountains. He was awarded the contract to build the road, which took about nine months to finish. This is where the Peter Kiewit & Sons construction company blasted for the Mule Pass Tunnel. This $2 million project was engineered by Ray Paulson. In today's money, that would be estimated to be $17.2 million, which was 87 percent funded by the federal government.

One of the main concerns and reasons behind the construction of the tunnel was that the Old Divide Road was a treacherous route with a reported six deaths and thirty-one cars towed. To this day, you can spot one or two rusted and rotting antique vehicles left behind in their original crash sites off the sharp cliffs along the road. These are unattainable for the tow trucks and left for eternity.

According to a 2018 article on the Arizona Department of Transportation (ADOT) Communications website, "Mule Pass Tunnel has eased trip to–from Bisbee for 60 years." It took 150 workers five months to complete it. They blasted and dug through 1,400 feet of granite to construct the tunnel to forty-two feet wide and twenty-three feet high. In all, 1,100 tons of steel and 15,000 cubic yards of concrete were used for this massive project. The dedication for the tunnel was held on December 19, 1958.

During the early Bisbee years, big conglomerates were always looking for ways to modernize and ease all styles of highway for better transportation of their goods. The New Mexico & Arizona Railroad built tracks from the new main Southern Pacific line in the town of Benson and then south to Fairbank, which was along the San Pedro River. Finally, in 1889, Phelps Dodge built the Arizona & Southeastern Railroad from Fairbank, all the way to Bisbee. In 1901, the El Paso & Southwestern Railroad Company bought the railway. This valuable extension to Bisbee was a huge factor in the increase in production of copper and other minerals.

After the railroad extension, the population increased, and a large economy emerged to support the influx of people. Railroad lines were being extended and connected for both freight and passenger services. Luckily for Bisbee residents, passenger services reached the new urban community.

In November 1903, an old freight train depot was dismantled to make room for a new passenger-freight combination depot. The five-stall roundhouse of crenelated sheet iron was located at the foot of OK Street. The overall length of the new depot was two hundred feet. The waiting room and ticket office were at the west end of the structure. On the site of the former roundhouse were the baggage and express offices. The part of the building that handled freight was on the spot where the turntable and lead tracks were previously located.

There were thirty windows on the second floor, giving the offices lots of sunlight. The two-story depot was completed on May 17, 1905. The passenger terminal opened to the public on June 24 and stayed open until 1951.

There were some horrendous train wrecks in Bisbee, but one is worth noting. In March 1902, two trains crashed in Lowell. At approximately 1:30 a.m., two engines from the El Paso & Southwestern Railway collided. Engine No. 8 was backing down from Bisbee with a caboose when it was run into by Engine No. 6. This happened on the curve of the track about one hundred

Brutal train wrecks were not uncommon in Bisbee. This one involved a brick wall in 1913. *Author's collection.*

yards from an electric plant. The caboose immediately caught fire, as did the superintendent's private car. The front end of No. 6 was badly crushed in.

Engine No. 8 had left just before 1:30 a.m. to do an extra run to Douglas. This train was given the right-of-way over No. 6. Local newspapers reported that when the train was just about to round the curve, Switch Conductor Marshall, who was seated in the cupola of the caboose, saw the headlight of the other train coming toward them. He had time only to jump and yell for everyone to do the same. Two brakemen, Lane and Woods, were able to jump off the rear of the train. A third brakeman, named Donahue, and a passenger, J. Kinneson, did not have time to jump and instead were thrown out of the top of the caboose from the force of the collision. Donahue was thrown on the upper side of the track and escaped with only bruises. Kinneson was thrown over the end of the caboose and was caught between it and the stack of the train's engine. Members of the railroad crew were able to save him before he could be burned to death.

When Conductor Marshall jumped off the train, he fell down the side of the grade thirty feet and, luckily, only cut one of his hands. Over on Engine No. 6, Engineer Gray and Fireman Erickbaum were left unharmed.

On impact, the trains blew up in a fiery ball. Just a few moments later, the train cars were also on fire. The same cupola Marshall had been sitting in moments before was torn off and hurled down the embankment, only to land a few feet from where he had landed.

It was reported that the trains were within one hundred feet of each other before Conductor Marshall shouted his warning. Superintendent Morgan reported that the cause of the wreck was the conductor failing to record orders to his register.

Another noteworthy fact about the town of Bisbee is that it had a military ship named after it. The USS *Bisbee* (PF-46) was a U.S. Navy Tacoma-class patrol frigate launched on September 7, 1943, by the Consolidated Steel Company shipyard in Los Angeles, California. The ship was commissioned on February 15, 1944. It was 303 feet, 11 inches long, had a top speed of twenty knots and required a crew of 190 to run it. It traveled the seas until February 13, 1952. The *Bisbee* received two battle stars for its participation in World War II and three for its service in Korea. In earnest, some believe that it was named after Bisbee as a gift of gratitude from the federal government for how much copper came out of the town's mines for the war effort during the First World War.

Panoramic view of Bisbee. *Courtesy Randy S. Powers.*

Bisbee was founded in 1880 and incorporated in 1902. In 1929, the county seat of Cochise County was changed from Tombstone to Bisbee. There are 2,300 miles of mine tunnels under Bisbee, Lowell and Warren. During Bisbee's mining period, more than three million ounces of gold and eight billion pounds of copper were extricated. The town's elevation is 5,300 feet. The original segment of Bisbee and its residential area became a historic district in 1980.

1

THE COPPER QUEEN LIBRARY

THE HANGING TREE

With the momentous success from the Bisbee mines came rugged and somewhat untamed citizens. Before Bisbee was considered a city of eloquence and a cosmopolitan community, it was packed with mostly single men, individuals looking for jobs with good pay or an outlet to make a fast dollar. In the late 1880s, the place to find a miner after his shift was in one of the many gambling and drinking establishments in town. One of these watering holes is where the Copper Queen Library got its precarious start.

According to an 1885 article in the *Weekly Champion*, a scene right out of the popular "spaghetti Western" genre occurred, involving a man called only a "Mexican Stranger." He was drinking heavily in the Bon Ton Saloon on Main Street on a Copper Queen payday. It was a Thursday evening, and the Stranger was inebriated. He was having a good time gambling and drinking until he decided to head over to a faro table occupied by several players.

The Stranger decided to play and leaned over a man's shoulder to do so. He then casually placed his elbow on the man. After several attempts made by the man to push the Stranger's arm off, he impatiently and aggressively threw it off. Without hesitation, the Stranger threw a punch, hitting the man. An all-out brawl ensued, ending with the Stranger being hit on the head with a chair. After that, the bartender grabbed him by the collar and threw him out on his ear.

Copper Queen
Library, circa 1920.
*Courtesy Copper Queen
Library.*

In the book *Bisbee, Not So Long Ago*, Opie Rundle Burgess writes that the Stranger immediately went to a friend's house to borrow his gun. He was rejected and decided to wait for his friend to go to sleep. The Stranger snatched the weapon and went directly back to the bar around four o'clock in the morning.

The Stranger stood behind the saloon's swinging door, then pushed through and opened fire on about thirty or forty men, many of whom were surrounding the same faro table as before. The same newspaper article stated that a bullet hit a man named Dave Hickey, who had just come into town from Tombstone. Hickey was shot in the jaw, and most of his upper lip was torn off. James Kehoe was shot in the left cheekbone. The bullet passed through his neck and traveled down his back. Witnesses stated that Kehoe was alive, lying on the floor for about twenty minutes before he died from his wounds.

A third slug passed through George Sales's left shoulder, and another hit a man named Jack Welch in the foot. Frank Gardiner was shot in the elbow. A total of fifteen shots were fired by the Stranger in rapid succession. The gunman left and headed to Pierce's Saloon and continued his ambuscade of vengeance. He fired two bullets through a glass door; luckily, no one was hit. After that, he headed toward a canyon and vanished into the night.

A posse was immediately organized, and according to Burgess, the gamblers targeted the Mexican Stranger as the suspect. Since a heavy storm had passed through Bisbee that same evening, the high desert's deep dust turned into thick mud. With the help of lanterns, the posse was able to follow the tracks of the shooter to his shack.

One of the earliest photos of Castle Rock and where the "hanging tree" was sited. *Author's collection.*

As soon as they reached the shack, they burst through the flimsy door and found the man they were looking for. He was on the floor, wrapped in a serape, asleep. Under the blanket they found the rifle, and they grabbed the Stranger's shoes to compare the tracks they had followed. There was enough evidence to prove he was indeed the assailant. In addition, the killer's friend verified that the rifle used in the crime was the one stolen from him earlier.

The Stranger was placed in jail overnight. With unwavering proof of his guilt and the power of the hand of the unwritten law of street justice, the following morning, he was led to his death. He was pulled with a rope around his neck to an oak tree at Castle Rock. One of the hanging tree's branches extended far out and over the road. The Mexican Stranger was hanged until dead from that limb. The killer was left swinging from the oak as an example of the town's intolerance of his acts of violence and a warning of what would happen to anyone who mirrored his actions.

Ben Williams, superintendent of the Copper Queen Mine, had gone to Tombstone the day of the shooting to pick up the company's directors from New York. These executives were said to be very excited to see the place that was producing the rich copper with such high dividends.

A fascinating view of the arches of Copper Queen Library. *Author's collection.*

They traveled by train to the Fairbank depot, then headed to Bisbee by stagecoach and arrived at night. The directors were impressed with the ride down the steep and rocky divide road, but when they reached Castle Rock, they saw the body of the dead man hanging from the big oak.

The next morning, without delay, the directors left Bisbee. Appalled by what they had seen and after a discussion on the train, they decided a more refined culture must be offered at the mining camp. Besides the street justice that took place, they did not like the heavy drinking and gambling and other entertainments being offered in town.

After collecting their heads to think of a way to bring distinguished values to the camp, the directors sent from New York a collection of between four hundred and five hundred books. These books were placed on shelves in the far corner of the Copper Queen Mercantile store.

This was the library for Bisbee until a two-story building was constructed. The library and the post office were on the ground floor; the second level

Castle Rock today. This photograph was taken at the same location as the photo with donkeys and firewood. *Author's collection.*

Holiday lights adorn the Copper Queen Library and the United States Post Office. *Courtesy David Day.*

was used as the Miner's Union Hall as well as for church services, dances and lodge meetings.

Reverend J.G. Pritchard became the first paid librarian in Bisbee in 1887 and was also the postmaster. That two-story library burned down in a devastating fire on Main Street in 1888. By 1892, a brick building had replaced it.

That building was torn down in 1906, and by March 1907, a three-story building had been constructed. It was the fourth building to house the library. The U.S. Post Office held 3,200 mailboxes by 1908. Since Bisbee's historic district neighborhoods are set in mountainous terrain, it is too difficult for a person to hand-deliver the mail, even today.

The Copper Queen Library was renovated with an elevator in 1997 to be handicap accessible and was named 2019's "Best Small Library in America" by *Library Journal*. This library was also the only one in Arizona to place along with thirty finalists for the National Medal for Museum and Library Service. The Copper Queen Library is the oldest continuously operating library in the state.

2

WILD AND WOOLY BISBEE

Shootouts and Murders

*L*aw in Mule Gulch (Bisbee) included Burton C. Mossman, who was the first Arizona Ranger captain. He was sworn into the position on August 30, 1901, and established the Ranger headquarters in Bisbee. He had been the superintendent of the Aztec Land and Cattle Company, which had sixty thousand head of cattle and a two-million-acre spread in northern Arizona near the towns of Holbrook and Winslow. Mossman spoke Spanish, was an especially good horseman and had great success in managing rustling for the cattle company. He is credited for the organizing and recruiting of the original Arizona Rangers and captured and killed a great number of outlaws. He retired in the summer of 1902 and went back to the cattle business.

There was another reliable personality who testified to everything wild and woolly in Bisbee in its earliest days. James Franklin Duncan was a Civil War veteran who was the representative for Cochise County, the commander of the Department of Arizona and a member of the Grand Army of the Republic (GAR). The GAR was a group of veterans of the Union army. Duncan, originally from Philadelphia, arrived in Arizona in 1879. He located to Mule Gulch and the following year was appointed justice of the peace. He was elected the next year and served in that position for eleven years. He was also very active in the First State Legislature on a variety of committees. Duncan made his home in Tombstone and died in Douglas in 1929. He is buried in that city cemetery.

A shootout reenactment depicting Bisbee's treacherous past. *Author's collection.*

In a special report given to the *Bisbee Daily Review* in 1911, Duncan gave his opinion about early Bisbee as a rough and tough place where certain individuals arrived with the notion that they might be able to continue their life of crime with no consequences. He said these men constituted one class and were known as rustlers. Then there were the good guys, who were willing to do anything in the name of justice, including murder. He described these men as making up the law-and-order party. Those in the high ranks he considered cowardly, because these men hired others to do the killing for them. If they were caught, their hands were clean.

Duncan described the United States Army as a government class of men who would only pass through the camp and were supposed to keep the various tribes of Apaches under control. They were also to help peace officers keep the "unruly" within bounds and on the right side of the law. Duncan complained that they seldom accomplished that mission.

Duncan stated: "From the foregoing, the people of Bisbee can have an idea what the early settlers of that now prosperous city had to contend with, and you can well understand how it came to pass. The prospectors and miners as a rule were of the law-and-order class and their goodness was show by their many acts of kindness toward their follow men."

Display set on an army blanket at the Cochise County Archives in Bisbee. McClellan cavalry saddle, circa late 1880s; replica 1800s cavalry saber, single-action U.S. Army Colt nonfiring replica; arm patch; U.S. Army recruiting poster; and dummy bullets. *Author's collection.*

He added that crime was low in Mule Gulch until the smelter opened. Duncan didn't actually blame the men who worked there, but as labor was needed, all sorts of characters found their way to the mining camp. He thought this was a result of heightened crime in the booming community.

What follows are four of his accounts of murders in the early days of the Bisbee mining camp.

FIRST MURDER

The mining camp was just digging its heels into organizing itself and becoming a civilized community. But in August of 1880, it appeared that civility hadn't yet shown its face. The first murder took place, and the killer got away with it.

Duncan reported that a young Mexican man, a laborer at the smelter, had come off his shift in the evening and went to an established restaurant located above Castle Rock. While eating his meal, a stranger to the residents of the camp shot and killed him. The stranger's intent was to kill the waitress serving the worker's table. The woman was shot but suffered only a flesh wound. The ball went straight through her and then hit the young man through his heart, killing him instantly. The victim had a piece of bread in his mouth when he perished. This was the first cold-blooded murder in the camp.

He was buried somewhere in Brewery Gulch. Duncan didn't specify if the man was buried in the pioneer cemetery, only that his grave was marked by a large wooden cross.

Murder over One Dollar

On the night of February 26, 1881, a man was assassinated over one dollar. A. Jordan, who was a saloonkeeper, and a man named Jack O'Brien had an unknown conflict. The victim was a man named Peter Hogan, who for some reason went to Jordan's saloon armed with a six-shooter.

Hogan went directly over to Jordan, who was standing behind the bar. Hogan told him he owed him a dollar. Jordan shrugged him off and said that if he did, he'd pay him but that he didn't recall anything about it. Even so, Jordan pulled out a dollar bill and gave it to Hogan. But Hogan wasn't satisfied. He told Jordan he now owed him two dollars.

Suddenly, a huge rock came crashing through the saloon's front window. It was thrown by O'Brien, who was standing outside. Jordan grabbed his shotgun off a shelf under the bar. Hogan started to shoot at Jordan, and Jordan returned fire. Hogan was shot in the left side of his head.

The camp's constable, George Bridge, was sitting by a stove in a corner of the room. Bridge went after Hogan, and the wounded man began to shoot at Bridge. Bridge grabbed Hogan by the arm and punched him. Bridge continued his attack, hitting Hogan on the head with his six-shooter just above where Jordan's bullet had hit. Hogan died two days later.

Several people were summoned to be witnesses or members of the coroner's jury at the inquest of the shooting on March 2. The jury's verdict stated that Hogan's death was caused by injuries sustained by Constable Bridge. A coroner's warrant was issued, and Bridge was arrested. Surprisingly, at the preliminary examination two days later, the witnesses now said just the opposite of what they originally stated.

After that, Bridge was exonerated of the charge made by the coroner's jury. Jordan faced no charges, as all testimony proved he was acting in self-defense.

A Man Named Daley

W.W. Lowther, the constable in April 1890, received a complaint about a man who had a bad reputation. Judge Petria issued a warrant for James Daley's arrest, and Lowther went to serve it. James Duncan warned Lowther that Daley was a dangerous man and that he shouldn't go alone to arrest him. Lowther laughed the comment off and left by himself.

Less than half an hour after Lowther left on his mission, Daley killed him. He left the scene and was not found. Duncan stated in March of the following year that he had stopped at a ranch six miles from Fort Bowie on the way back from an overnight trip he had taken nearby. He had just stabled his horse and was walking back to the ranch house. As he walked on the path and passed a large boulder, Daley popped out from behind it. Duncan said that this startled and surprised him, as he had no idea Daley was still in the territory.

The murderer told Duncan not to be afraid. Duncan said he wasn't but confessed later that night that he was. Daley said he knew who his friends were as he stared into the constable's eyes. Duncan asked him what he was doing there and promised he was surely going to be arrested.

Daley only smirked and didn't answer any of the constable's questions. Duncan concluded that he was staying somewhere close, as he was clean and didn't appear tired from traveling. Apparently, Duncan didn't arrest Daley that day, because he said he never knew what became of him after their strange meeting. He only heard a rumor that Daley died in California.

Lucky Day for Dan Simons

On a September morning in 1887, Joseph Smith, a known cowboy, went into the Clark and Letson saloon. As soon as he entered, he began to shoot at the floor. A constable named Dan Simons was at a table and immediately rushed to stop him. Smith took a shot at Simons. The ball missed his body and only went through the man's vest. Simons returned fire and shot Smith, killing him instantly.

Simons was acquitted of any charges, as it was determined that he had acted in self-defense.

MORE SHOOTINGS

The Bisbee Massacre

Sadly, a long list of shootings and murders pepper the wicked side of Bisbee's past. But there is one torrid event that is very prominent in the town's history. This is the Bisbee Massacre.

During the winter season, Bisbee can be dusted with snow. On the morning of December 8, 1883, in this bustling mining camp, a heavy snowfall blanketed the entire community. The snow had been falling the entire first week of December. That serene picture absolutely shifted to a tragic scene: an unholy and bloody massacre. That cold evening at 7:00 p.m., five strangers attempted to rob the only safe in town with the expectation of grabbing $7,000 in payroll money. Four people, plus an unborn child, were murdered during the massacre.

Bisbee's Main Street in 1883 was a long and narrow dirt road, about eighteen feet wide—perhaps just enough room for two wagons to pass each other. Buildings on the street were made mostly of wood and were tightly fitted on either side of the street. Letson Block is the name of the site of two buildings that are recorded as the oldest on Main Street. It is also the site of the Bisbee Massacre.

In 1888, James Letson erected the Mansion House Hotel, an adobe building on the left. On the right, he built the Turf Saloon in 1894. Before the Letson Block was built, the Goldwater-Castañeda Store stood at that location. The Bon Ton Saloon was next to the Letson Hotel, in front of what is now 28 Main Street. The Goldwater-Castañeda Store is where 22 and 24 Main Street are today. Across the street is where the Hardy's Store used to stand (23 Main Street). The owner left town suddenly, leaving the store vacant for a man named John Heath (sometimes spelled "Heith") to move in. He opened a dance hall there, according to James F. Duncan of Tombstone, a witness to the massacre.

Left: Site of the Bisbee Massacre on Main Street and where five men killed four innocent citizens, including an unborn child, during a robbery gone wrong. *Author's collection.*

Below: Looking down Main Street and where the bandits would have walked up to the Goldwater-Castañeda Store. *Author's collection.*

Some historians say that his dance hall was not there but instead at 38 Main. At today's 29 Main, Annie Roberts owned the Bisbee Hotel that was adjoined to two saloons. Bill Daniels owned one, and William Roberts owned the other.

During the first week of December, five strangers were seen loitering around town, keeping a low profile. But on that dark evening, the same men made their way to Main Street. With masks on their faces, they bent over and crept up the street after tying their horses at Preston's Lumberyard, near where the library and post office are today.

From there, they made their way to the Goldwater Castañeda Store on the same side of the street. Two of the men, Dan Dowd, and Billy Delaney, stationed themselves on the sidewalk at the entrance to the store. A delivery wagon was parked in front. Dan Kelly, Red Sample and Tex Howard entered the store. As soon as they entered, they yelled for everyone inside to put their hands in the air. José Miguel Castañeda, the manager, was at the back of the store near a bedroom door. Thinking fast, he grabbed several hundred dollars and went into the back room. He placed the money under a pillow and lay down on the bed and faked being sick.

Tex Howard followed him and screamed and pushed at him to get up. Then he took the cash and shoved Castañeda back into the store. Meanwhile, Red Sample made Joe Goldwater open the safe. Sample told Goldwater, "Get the payroll." Goldwater answered: "That's where you're fooled. The stagecoach is late. The money is not here." Sample pushed Goldwater aside and helped himself to Mexican money and valuables belonging to several Bisbee residents.

Outside, two Bisbee men, John C. Tappenier and Joseph Bright, came out of the Bon Ton Saloon and started to pass Dowd and Delaney as they walked up the street. Delaney commanded the two men to go into the store. Tappenier refused and turned to go back to the saloon. Bright started to run up the street, Dowd firing after him. Delaney's first shot missed Tappenier, but the second shot hit him in the head, tearing away a portion of his skull and leaving his brains running off the porch of the Bon Ton Saloon, where he fell. "Johnny" Tappenier was in his early twenties at this time and was a miner with Austria roots.

While this was happening, a volunteer fireman named James Krigbaum and some others ran out of the alley between the bank building at 5 Main and started shooting at the bandits. Krigbaum took aim at one of the tall outlaws and fired, grazing his coat.

At this time, a deputy from New Mexico named Tom Smith was with his wife eating a meal in Manuel Sima's restaurant (25 Main Street). Deputy

Smith came out, ordered them to quit shooting and told them that he was a lawman. Delaney said, "You're the man we're lookin for." He then shot Smith in the left shoulder. Deputy Smith remarked, "I am hit." Delaney said, "I will give you another." The second shot killed Smith. The deputy's body was found between the shafts of a delivery wagon. After being shot the second time, Smith crawled through from the back of the wagon and died.

An eight-months-pregnant Annie Roberts was standing at her door when the shooting began. She came out to peek at what was causing the commotion outside. When she turned to go back to the building, one of the balls from Dowd's gun missed Bright and passed through the doorjamb, then lodge in the small of her back. Some historians write that the young woman was standing in front of a window of her hotel when the bandit saw the shadow of a person and shot through the glass. Roberts died in terrible agony the next morning.

J.A. Nolly was in a saloon (21 Main) when the shooting started. He ran out and was shot by Dowd in the belly. Nolly died the following week. The gang managed to get out of town while two Bisbee men, Bill Daniels and John Reynolds, ran down the gulch with guns blazing, chasing the bandits. They didn't manage to hit a single target. The Bisbee Massacre lasted a total of about fifteen minutes.

Immediately, Krigbaum was sent to Tombstone for help. The *Bisbee Review* reported that he made it there on his horse in about two hours. Ironically, on the way there, he passed the stagecoach with the $7,000 the gang was after.

A vigilante group of between forty-five and fifty Bisbee men was organized the same night. Daniels and John Heath were part of the search party. Before dawn, they heard of the death of Mrs. Roberts and her unborn child. This was the last straw of bad news and kicked the posse into a mode of retribution and pure vengeance.

When the party reached a fork in the road at Forest Ranch, Heath tried to convince the others that the gang must be heading north toward the Dragoons or even Tombstone. The others disagreed strongly and headed to Sulphur Springs Valley and the Chiricahua Mountains instead. Heath went north. The posse was on the gang's trail, which led them to the ranch of Dan Ross. Near the Ross house, there was a large crevice in the rock, twenty to twenty-five feet deep. Here the posse found the carcasses of horses. They had been run almost to death. The bandits stripped them of their bridles and saddles and brutally shoved them into the crevice, leaving them there to die. The outlaws then walked, carrying their saddles and bridles, into the ranch of Frank Buckles, where they camped for several days before stealing his horses.

After the appalling discovery, the posse continued trekking and stopped at the cabin of Luben Pardu. Pardu said that five men stopped at his place, divided up some money and items and then left in different directions. He also said that another man and the same group had been at his cabin a week before. The other man seemed to act like the leader of the group. He named all five men, plus John Heath as their leader. Heath was quickly found in Bisbee and taken to Tombstone.

Months later, all of the men were caught. On February 8, 1884, the defendants were brought into court to make their pleas. Each pleaded not guilty. Heath was tried alone. On February 17 at 8:00 p.m., the jurors gave Heath the verdict of guilty of murder in the second degree. On February 21, John Heath was led into court and given the sentence of serving for life at the territorial prison in Yuma for his participation in the Bisbee Massacre.

Several Bisbee citizens were worried that he would live long enough to be pardoned. They decided to take the law into their own hands to avoid the possibility that Heath would take his case to the U.S. Supreme Court. This Committee of Safety, called "45/60," announced that "John Heath was guilty as hell and deserved the same punishment as the others."

On the morning of February 22, the committee, made up of some of the most influential Bisbee citizens and miners, traveled to Tombstone and at 8:00 a.m. marched to the jail unmasked. They were met by men from the Contention and the Grand Central Mines. At that point, seven men from Bisbee went to the door leading to the jail and knocked, yelling to let them in. Two men kicked at the jail's gate, and chief jailer Will Jerome Ward opened the door on their demand. The jailer was expecting breakfast for the prisoners at that time and answered unarmed. Instantly, he was staring into numerous gun barrels and was ordered to hand over the keys. Ward didn't resist and handed them over. The men opened Heath's cell, unshackled him and led him out into a hall of the jail. They grabbed Heath, and a rope held by several men was placed around his waist. It was reported that the group's first intention was to hang him immediately from the banister of the stairs leading to the second story of the jail building, but the larger part of the crowd was already heading to a telegraph pole just a little farther up the road.

As Heath and the crowd got to the front of the door of the courthouse, they were met by Sheriff Jerome L. Ward, who began shouting in a strong voice of authority: "Stop this! You have got to stop this right here!" The sheriff was the father of the chief jailer.

Without hesitation, the sheriff was picked up and thrown down the stairs by an unidentified individual as the crowd continued with its mission.

John Heath hangs from a telegraph pole in Tombstone after a Bisbee mob set its version of "street justice" into action. *Author's collection.*

They dragged Heath and ran down Toughnut Street to a point below where the railroad crosses the street. The rope was then hung on the telegraph pole.

Witnesses said that on arriving at the site, Heath pulled a handkerchief from his pocket and said these words: "Boys, you are hanging an innocent man, and you will find it out before those other men are hung. Tie this handkerchief over my eyes. I am not afraid to die. I have one favor to ask, that you will not mutilate my body by shooting into it after I am hung." His request was followed, and his eyes were covered; in an instant, he was strung up and was dead. His body was left dangling from the rope hanging from the crossbar on the telegraph pole. His body hung there for many hours before

John Heath plaque at Toughnut Street in Tombstone memorializing the hanging of the man who was the "mastermind" of the Bisbee Massacre. *Author's collection.*

it was taken down and sent to the office of the county physician, Dr. George Goodfellow. Heath's death certificate reads, "John Heath came to his death from emphysema of the lungs, a disease common in high altitudes, which might have been caused by strangulation, self-inflicted or otherwise."

On February 19, 1884, the five bandits were sentenced for the murders, and on March 25, each was hanged by the neck until dead. The graves of the five members of the gang are in the Boothill Cemetery in Tombstone; there is also a marker for Heath, but he is interred in Terrell, Texas, and was returned to his family and to his father, who was a farmer in Kaufman County.

Heath was well known and mentioned in several Texas newspapers regarding his situation in Bisbee, Arizona, and having a long criminal history. He was mentioned as having a wayward disposition and was frequently able to manage to escape punishment. It may have been his gift of gab and his charismatic personality that helped, but Texans said they knew him personally and regarded him as a desperate character. In the *Fort Worth Daily Gazette* newspaper, a blurb reported that Heath was a notorious Dallas character who had been arrested over twenty times and had been confined in the county jail on charges of horse and cattle stealing, burglary and other crimes. Again, it was mentioned that he seemed to always succeed in dodging any kind of final conviction and punishment for his criminalities. One could suppose that he finally ran out of luck on that cold February day in Tombstone.

According to the *Herald* newspaper in an announcement about Heath's hanging printed on February 28, 1884, a place card was posted on the telegraph pole where his body was found. The card had the following inscription: "John Heith was hanged to this pole by the Citizens of Cochise County for participation in the Bisbee massacre as a proved accessory at 8:20 A.M., February 22, 1884 (Washington's Birthday)."

The Unsolved Murder of Nat Anderson

A unique building stands in the heart of the historic district of Bisbee that since 1920 has held a murder mystery that still has not been solved. The Oliver House is the site of the killing of a man named Nat Anderson. He was brutally shot at close range. Despite any forensic investigations that took place, the killer was never named.

Over the years, the Oliver House was used as a mining office and, during the Depression, a men's dormitory.

Jane Oliver, the original owner, ran the inn by herself until her death in 1912. Her son Richard Davis and his wife, Lilly Belle, took over. During this time, an unmarried roadmaster for the Copper Queen Mining Company was shot there on February 22, 1920. The shooting was called the "Oliver House Notorious Murder."

According to the *Bisbee Daily Review*, Nat Anderson was gunned down by an unknown assailant as he was entering his room in the Oliver lodging house at around 3:30 a.m. He died at the Copper Queen Hospital at 1:20 p.m. the same day without regaining consciousness. He had been a roadmaster for two years at the mining company on Sacramento Hill.

A detailed description of the murder was released by the police. The first shot probably killed Anderson, as he was struck in the forehead. As he fell, the second bullet hit his chest, causing a severe flesh wound but never entering his body. As Anderson lay flat on his face, his killer fired a third bullet into the lower part of his back.

Lilly Belle Davis reported to police that the sound of three gunshots woke her up as Anderson got to the top of the stairs to his room on the second floor. She said she heard a man's voice that wasn't Anderson's hurl a violent obscenity at the time of the shooting, as though in overwhelming anger. She

The Oliver House sits quietly now, but it holds history regarding a murder mystery that has never been solved. *Author's collection.*

ran into the hall and saw a stranger run down the stairs and into the street but could not give a good description to police.

Kay Ross, by trade a timekeeper at the Sacramento Mine, was a tenant at the lodging house. He heard the shooting from his bed. He got up and grabbed his gun and peered into the hall. He saw Anderson lying on the stairway, close to the door of his room. No one else was in sight.

Shortly after, policeman Tex Barton appeared on the scene. Ross told Bisbee police that he had known Anderson for several years and said his friend had a reputation of drinking very little and of having good habits. In addition, Anderson was liked by many. Ross couldn't think of and knew no motive. It was known that Anderson had attended a house party just before he was murdered. Police retraced his footsteps between the time he left the party at midnight and the time when he was shot.

The article in the *Bisbee Daily Review*, "Murder of Anderson Baffles Police; Roadmaster Shot in Hall of Rooming House Dies," states that Ross discovered that he had been robbed. The authorities immediately believed that the person who robbed Ross's room shot Anderson because the assailant was surprised by his appearance. The police investigated further and argued that it would be unusual for a petty thief to shoot and kill someone. They instead figured that the mode of Anderson's murder pointed to a personal grudge, not to a thief attempting to get away.

When Ross went back into his room, he noticed that his wallet was on the floor near the door. He called police and said that twenty-five dollars was missing. Ross went to the police station the following morning to report that his watch was also gone.

In Ross's statement to police, he said he had worked the night shift and gone to bed approximately an hour before the shooting took place. The timekeeper stated that he had a routine of taking any items from his pockets and putting them on the dresser. He concluded that all a person had to have done was go into his room, grab his things and leave. He thought the thief took the money from his wallet under the light of the hall and, on leaving, put it on the floor near the door.

Even though Ross initially thought that the person who stole from him was also the killer, he changed his mind. He said that by the way Anderson died he figured the killing was the result of a personal vendetta.

The article "Find No Clues to Killing of Nat Anderson" in the *Tombstone Epitaph* stated that investigators found out that Anderson was at a party held by the wife of Norris Greely in the neighborhood of Wood Canyon. He was there until approximately 1:00 a.m. on the night of his death. It was reported that the party was a gathering of friends playing cards and dancing. The guests left at the same time and walked together for a short distance before Anderson supposedly separated from the group with a young woman named Elizabeth King. He walked her to her residence on Temby Avenue.

He visited with King at her home and left at approximately 2:25 a.m. After that, he walked down to Main Street, where he ate at the English

The same bridge today and where a woman's scream was heard before the shooting. *Author's collection.*

Kitchen. Authorities report that he left the restaurant shortly after his meal and then went directly to the Oliver House. A neighbor came forward and stated that on the wooden footbridge that crosses a path to the yard of the Oliver House she heard some sort of scuffle and a woman's scream before the shooting. A decision made at an inquest hearing held on February 28 by a coroner's jury gave a verdict of "death from gunshot wounds at the hands of an unknown person."

As the investigation went on, authorities said that Ross's robbery may have been a coincidence, or the killer was trying to throw them off the trail to make it look like the thief was only trying to escape.

A notice ran in the *Bisbee Daily Review* for about three weeks with a $500 reward from the Moose Lodge for the arrest and conviction of Anderson's murderer.

According to his death certificate, Anderson was born in 1882 and his cause of death was a gunshot wound to his forehead. He had a sister in Utica, Mississippi. Funeral services for Anderson were held at the Palace Undertaking Parlor on February 25, 1920, under the auspices of the same lodge. His body was shipped to Mississippi.

Lowell Deputy Shoots Miner in Cold Blood

On October 4, 1919, at the St. Regis Hotel in Lowell, Sheriff Deputy Otto Laine deliberately shot a Bisbee miner named Tony Rimac in cold blood and recklessly wounded five innocent bystanders. The lead-up to the shooting was a two-year-long tension between Rimac and some local members of the Industrial Workers of the World (IWW). The miner worked at the Lowell Shaft and was targeted with harassment and disparaged for most of the time he worked in Bisbee. He was from Slavonia and was a steady worker in the Warren District for three years, working at the Lowell Shaft the longest.

Rimac had a reputation for being a law-abiding citizen and for keeping to himself. But he was still regularly tormented at work and even on the streets. The phrase he was most often called was a "gun-toting scab." The man was so bothered and stressed that he asked for protection for more than a month from the chief watchman for the Calumet and Arizona Mining Company (C&A), Billy Woods, and from the foreman of the Junction Mine, Fred Santner. Rimac eventually decided to quit and bought a train ticket to El Paso.

Several witnesses stated that on the night before Rimac was going to leave town, he was being harassed by the same men in the billiard area of the hotel. It was somehow known that Rimac usually carried a lot of cash. That evening, he was carrying $435. The men harassing him tried to talk Rimac into staying for another day or two to donate to their carousing. He declined

Lowell at one time had scandal, murder and Wild West shootouts. *Author's collection.*

their offer. The miners didn't like that response, so they surrounded him near the pool table and started to swing and poke their cues at him. They also threw pool balls at him. Some missing Rimac and broke a large-paned window of the hotel, adding the sound of shattered glass to the chaos.

Rimac drew a pocketknife with a four-inch blade and lunged at one of the tyrants, Nick Pesha, who was also Slavonian. Rimac cut Pesha, giving him a flesh wound along his ribs, then decided to head for the door. On his way out, he slashed his knife at the vicious group, slightly wounding three more men. He cut Emil Bouteras, George Pilj and Ely Radmanovich and cut a hole in the shirt of George Balen. In all the commotion, a crowd of spectators formed around Rimac as he stood near the front of the room; the men he wounded were crouched in the back.

A stranger walked calmly up to Rimac and asked what was going on. The man spoke very few words to him. Rimac said he wasn't going to hurt anyone with the knife, which was still in his hand.

Suddenly, Deputy Laine, dressed in regular street clothes and wearing no law enforcement badge, rushed into the building. He was the caretaker of Finnish Hall, located across from the hotel and acknowledged as IWW headquarters. He grabbed a liquor bottle and hit Rimac across his face, making a deep cut along the checkbone. Rimac lunged at the deputy, but the lawman spun around and ran outside and across the street to Finnish Hall.

Within seconds, Laine rushed back in carrying a .35-calibre automatic revolver while clumsily pinning a deputy sheriff's badge onto his vest. Laine had not informed Rimac that he was an officer and that he was trying to place him under arrest. Rimac had no idea that months before, Laine was deputized by Sheriff McDonald.

With the gun in his hand, Laine began to walk toward Rimac. The miner stepped toward him, then the deputy spun around and made his way to the sidewalk outside, where he turned back toward Rimac and opened fire, shooting him. The first shot struck Rimac through the right thigh and just below his groin. At this point, there were approximately two hundred people in and around the hotel. Witnesses said that they saw Rimac stagger as the bullet hit him. He stumbled to the curb and plopped himself down.

As the injured man sat, he was breathing heavily and holding his gunshot wound while Deputy Laine walked toward him. He told Rimac to give him the knife. The wounded miner, dazed by the loss of blood, turned awkwardly toward the deputy. As Rimac slightly put his hand on the ground to support himself, Laine shot him again repeatedly, as if he was possessed with an anger that could only be satisfied with the death of the miner.

Rimac was hit two more times. As the bullets flew, they also hit bystanders in the crowd. Four innocent people were shot. One person was shot through the kneecap, and another person was hit through the upper part of the thigh, smashing the bone. Another person was shot in the hand. Yet another spectator was shot, but miraculously, the bullet was stopped by the clasp of his belt.

Finally, Laine's gun was emptied, and Rimac was bleeding heavily from six holes where the three bullets had entered and exited. As Rimac lay there, Laine went back into the hotel and escaped to the second floor as people screamed for help. No officer was to be found. Judge J.L. Winter, who was in his office nearby, ran to the hotel. He was told where the deputy was and placed him under arrest. At first, Laine resisted, but then he gave up and was taken to jail.

Rimac was taken to the C&A by ambulance and was thought to recover. Sheriff McDonald was in Tombstone at the time of the shooting but was able to visit with Rimac the same night. After talking with the miner, McDonald drove to the jail and released Laine.

As soon as Laine was let go, he said he wanted a larger gun. He said the .32-caliber revolver wasn't big enough for a deputy sheriff to use while trying to keep a man from killing others. He did not mention to the sheriff that his victim was weak, injured and confused and that Laine could have easily arrested him. The sheriff seemed unconcerned about the incident and left for Gleeson that night. He made this statement to local newspaper reporters: "Laine was perfectly justified in what he had done."

In the hospital, Rimac said that the men he fought off in the hotel had been making his life miserable and attacked him because he wouldn't do what they wanted. He said he asked for protection because of the many threats the men had made in the month before the incident. He said: "I know all the men who assaulted me in the pool room. I have known them for a long time." Through their investigation of the shooting, authorities were able to verify Rimac's claim for protection from the C&A.

Remember Nick Pesha, one of the men attacking Rimac? He was being treated for his knife wound in the same hospital and told Deputy Mert Gilman when questioned that he did not know the miner. After a few questions from the deputy, Pesha contradicted himself. He was forced to tell the truth and said he had known Rimac for over a year.

A report circulated that proclaimed Rimac to be mentally ill. The two deputies said they had spoken to the miner and that he was of sound mind during the interview. Rimac argued against his arrest, saying he had done nothing wrong but that he was willing to be seen by Dr. E.B Walker for an examination of his mental state.

The doctor and two deputies had the opinion that Rimac was perfectly sane and was a peaceful and hardworking miner who had enjoyed this reputation for his three years in Bisbee.

Not even a week after the shooting, the county attorney filed a charge of assault with intent to kill against Deputy Laine. The case was filed with Judge J.L. Winters of Lowell. Laine's bond was $2,000.

At that time, Rimac was recovering rapidly, despite a bullet having gone through his right lung and a thigh. Dr. E. Darragh repaired those injuries and also removed a bullet from Rimac's arm. The rest of the injured men were also free from any degree of peril.

The preliminary hearing for Deputy Laine was pushed back two weeks from its original date. Judge Winters postponed the date because he wanted Rimac and the other injured witnesses to be present to testify. At the hearing, it was decided that Laine would remain in the custody of the sheriff's office. His bond was now $5,000. The case headed to the Arizona Superior Court.

Many residents from Bisbee went to Tombstone to attend the trial on November 7 in the case of the State of Arizona v. Otto Laine. Twelve jurors gave the court a verdict of not guilty after only six minutes of deliberation. The jurors stated that the main reason they decided to acquit Laine was that Rimac refused to testify. They also said this verdict was the only possible one that could be reached.

3

MURDER, SUICIDE AND ADULTERY

THE JOHNSON ADDITION MASSACRE

Bisbee's landscape has drastically changed since the town was incorporated in 1902. For instance, there used to be an entire neighborhood where the Lavender Pit is now located. The mining company always found new and progressive ways to gain more ore, so in 1917, Bisbee's first "open pit" was created. The Sacramento Pit was not very lucrative and closed in 1929. The company didn't give up on the idea; in 1954, another open pit was produced. The Lavender Pit is the one you see today. It was much more productive and didn't close until 1975. The pit was named after Harry Lavender, a general manager of the Copper Queen Branch. He died before the pit began production.

Of course, for these open pits to exist, houses on the property had to be moved before blasting. These houses were relocated to surrounding neighborhoods, such as Galena, near the Warren area. The houses were built on stilts, not on foundations.

An area near upper Lowell was known as the Johnson Addition. It was heavily populated by miners and their families. On April 1, 1940, in this neighborhood, a husband killed his wife and two men, attempted to kill another woman but failed and then committed suicide.

Howard H. Trahern was a salesman who was out of work and had recently separated from his wife, Iter, who was known to occasionally wait tables around town. Iter had left her husband two weeks before the incident. The

Sacramento Hill, 1917. *Author's collection.*

Traherns had a twelve-year-old daughter at the time and had lived in the Johnson Addition neighborhood for two years. Iter was apparently staying with a divorced miner named Roy Sanders on the night before the killings. He lived across from the Traherns in an apartment house. A married couple, Charles and Helen Cloud, lived next door to Sanders.

According to a *Tucson Daily Citizen* article, "Three Killed by Bisbee Man," at 6:00 a.m., Howard walked across the street to Sanders's apartment. He made his way to the man's bedroom and saw his wife and Sanders asleep in bed with an empty whiskey bottle on a pillow between them. He pointed his gun at the two and shot each in the head.

The Clouds heard the gunfire, and Charles investigated while Helen remained in their apartment. As Howard was leaving Sander's apartment, he ran into Charles. Coroner L.T. Frazier stated that there must have been a struggle between the two men. Evidently, Charles attempted to take the revolver from Howard, but when he did, he was shot twice in the chest. The *Arizona Republic* reported that Mrs. Cloud heard the gunshots and ran to the apartment. She said that Howard aimed the gun at her, but the weapon failed to discharge.

Coroner Frazier reported that Trahern turned from Mrs. Cloud and then ran across the street to his home, where he shot himself in the heart seconds before Bisbee police officers arrived. Howard had the gun clutched in his hand when his body was found. The coroner said he had no fingers on his right hand and only two fingers and a thumb on his left hand. The theory is that he held the revolver with his two fingers and thumb and operated the trigger with the palm of his right hand.

An incredible sight when Sacramento Hill was destroyed with dynamite for the new open pit for its new surface mining. *Author's collection.*

Helen told the coroner that she believed Iter and Sanders were still breathing when she found the bodies. Later, a doctor disagreed and said the two must have been killed almost instantly. Coroner Frazier said that during his investigation he couldn't find out when Iter had arrived at Sanders' residence, but the beds in her and her husband's home had been occupied the same evening. The coroner was trying to learn where Howard, Iter and Sanders had been earlier in the night. Witnesses said that the Traherns' young daughter was seen running and screaming from her home after her father killed himself.

Iter Trahern's death certificate reports that she was originally from Arkansas and was forty-four. Her cause of death was a gunshot through her left temple. Sanders's death certificate states that he was originally from Oklahoma and was forty-eight at the time of his murder. He died from a gunshot through his left cheek that traveled into his brain.

Charles Cloud's death certificate gives his age as thirty-four when he was shot through the upper part of his chest and through his lungs. He was also from Oklahoma.

His death certificate states that he was forty-six and committed suicide with a gunshot through his heart. His time of death was at 6:40 a.m. Howard was another Oklahoman. All death certificates also state the murders and suicide took place in the Johnson Addition neighborhood.

HUSBAND KILLS RIVAL WITH SHOTGUN

J.D. Lee was a carpenter employed in Globe. On Election Day in 1906, he shot and killed Jack "Boss" Davis with a double-barreled shotgun. Mr. Lee fired two shots, and the thirty-two-year-old Davis died instantly. Lee had heard that Davis had been intimate with his wife, Hattie, who already had a promiscuous reputation in Lowell. Lee had also heard that his wife had encouraged Davis to kill him. According to an article in the *Bisbee Daily Review*, "Husband Kills Rival with Shot Gun," the homicide happened near Main Street in Lowell.

An investigation of the killing found that Davis had walked up the path that led to the Lee house and, as he made his way closer and came around the corner of the McBride home next door, Lee literally blew his head off. The bullets from the subsequent shots went into the neighbor's house, indicating that Lee had changed his position before firing again. Mrs. McBride was inside her home at the time, and the shooting was just outside her door. The dead body fell into the little yard of the McBride residence. The man's head landed almost in the doorway of the house, which was riddled with buckshot.

The shooting was easily heard from Lowell, and almost immediately a deputy sheriff appeared at the scene. The deputy met Mr. Lee as he was coming down the path that led to town. The shooter gave himself up to the officer and was placed under arrest. He was taken to the Cochise County Branch Jail in Bisbee. Lee made a statement to the *Bisbee Daily Review* the same day. When asked why he killed Davis, Lee said: "I had to do it in self-defense. When he came around the house, he had a six-shooter in his hand and was in the act of raising it when I fired the first shot."

The first officers on the scene found Davis's gun lying between his legs. Lee had repeatedly said he was forced to kill Davis or be killed himself. He also said that on his return from Globe, he heard that Davis had intended to kill him. Lee also admitted that he carried the shotgun anytime he was in his yard and in his home for protection and never went anywhere without it. Lee said that when he left for Globe, his wife had Davis as a boarder. He also shared some dirt on Davis, claiming that Davis went under the name Chas Drain in Roswell, New Mexico, and had at one time been in a penitentiary in Santa Fe, New Mexico.

On J.D. Lee's return from Globe, Hattie Lee left and went to stay with a married couple with the last name Fuss in Brewery Gulch because she was afraid of her husband. When Davis was killed, Hattie was at the Fuss's house,

The Cochise County Branch Jail held the most controversial and brutal criminals during Bisbee's heyday. *Author's collection.*

but later in the day she did go to Lowell to view the body, but not to the jail to see her husband. The couple were married in Mexico but remarried in Bisbee about a year before the shooting. According to statements made by an array of people, the infidelity by both of them started at that time. The woman had filed for divorce, but it was denied by the court.

Mrs. McBride gave an account of what happened, sharing it with the *Bisbee Daily Review* on the same day the murder took place. She stated that J.D. Lee had told her earlier that morning that if he saw Davis, he would kill him. She told him that there better be no shooting near her house and to go farther up the hill if there was going to be any sort of trouble. She added that she had invited Davis to her house that afternoon for lunch, as he had been a close friend of her and her husband. So she sent her young son to town with a note warning Davis about Lee's threat. The boy handed Davis the note and told him that Lee had been standing near his fence at home when he left and that he heard Lee say he was going to kill Davis if he was anywhere near there.

Mrs. McBride reported that just as her son returned she heard Lee say, "Here he comes now." She knew there was going to be a serious problem. She said she never saw Davis walking up but knew it was him when Lee made that comment. The distraught woman said she and her son went into the house and began screaming as soon as the first shot was fired and made her house vibrate. She ran to the other side of the home and with her son jumped through the window and tore through the screen.

The same reporter approached Mrs. Lee at the Fuss residence in Brewery Gulch for an interview later that day. Hattie Lee was crying when she began her own version of the incident. Her statement is as follows:

> "I want to have justice done and I am going to have it. My husband had no right to kill that man any more than he would have to kill you." She was asked about the rumor going around Lowell that she had been on intimate terms with Davis, she replied, "Then they lie, and I defy them to prove the assertion. Besides Davis, I had other boarders at my house and had to support myself for the past year. My husband has not contributed one penny towards my support during this time.
>
> "I refused to stay in the same house with him because I was afraid of him. He drank a great deal. I would not stay in the house at night and have been sleeping here at the home of Mr. and Mrs. Fuss. When he came to the house with the shotgun, I sent word to my brother not to come near the place for I was afraid that he would kill him."

MURDER, SUICIDE AND ADULTERY

In an interview with the *Arizona Silver Belt* newspaper, Hattie Lee claimed that her husband's real name was W.R. Leake. Hattie said that she was very bitter toward her husband and said she would appear against him in court. In the same article, Mr. Lee said that the Davis man had caused trouble for him and his wife before. He said he had been away at Globe for a long time and that when he returned he found Davis in his house. Lee told Davis to leave and to not come back.

He added more to the account of the shooting and said that as Davis stepped around the corner of the McBride house, Davis drew his gun to get the first shot. That's when he let him have both barrels. "I had to shoot," claimed Lee.

Court documents indicate that the three same individuals had been in court before. One of the reports stated that Davis had J.D. Lee arrested for stealing a horse, something Hattie Lee claimed.

J.D. Lee mentioned in the *Silver Belt* interview that the spring before the shooting, Davis had him arrested for horse stealing. The horse was proven in the end to be Lee's property, making the arrest unlawful and for the complainant to be malice in his actions. After that, it appeared that a game of charges and countercharges took place between the men, causing a larger rift between them. Davis left town for Mexico for a while but returned when Lee was in Globe. Davis returned to Lowell on Election Day to vote, but a diversion to possibly see Hattie Lee was the biggest mistake of his life.

J.D. Lee was indicted for murder and returned to Globe several months after the shooting and was released on bail. In December 1907, at the end of the trial in the case of *Territory of Arizona v. J.D. Lee*, the defendant was released from the charge of murder and found not guilty.

THE GEORGE CARSON STORY

There are people whom drama seems to follow. One person in particular was a magnet for it. Hattie Lee, whose husband shot and killed Jack Davis, found herself in another bloody mix-up. On May 23, 1907, another lover of hers, a Texan named George Carson, was killed by R.G. McBride. Ironically, he had used a shotgun. Reports stated that reasons for the shooting extended back to the death of Davis. McBride said that he shot Carson because of the threats he had made and the vile insults he had thrown at Mrs. McBride.

51

Does the name *McBride* sound familiar? It belongs to the same couple who lived next door to the Lees and in whose yard Davis's head had fallen. They were also part of the investigation of the Davis murder but now were in a squabble with Hattie Lee. Lee's husband had left her and skipped town at this point. Mrs. McBride was again a star witness. According to a *Bisbee Daily Review* article, "Lee Woman Is Involved in Murder," the shooting site was almost the same location as the last one, near Main Street in Lowell.

Witnesses reported being startled by a shot at midmorning, and several people ran to where the sound came from. They found Carson wallowing in his own blood; an entire side of his face had been blown off. At the same time, Mr. McBride was walking back to his house with a shotgun in his hands. A few minutes later, Officers George Gray and Harvey Hughes arrived and arrested McBride and had Carson rushed to the Calumet & Arizona Hospital. He died at 4:30 p.m. the same afternoon.

A short time after Mr. McBride was taken to the Cochise County Branch Jail in Bisbee, Hattie Lee went to Judge Grier's office in Lowell. She filed a complaint charge of first-degree murder against Mr. McBride. She also filed a charge against Mrs. McBride for threatening to kill her.

About one hour later, Mrs. McBride was brought into court and was released on a $500 bond. She paid the fee and immediately turned around and went to file her own complaint charges against Hattie Lee. She charged her with arson and said that Lee had threatened to kill her. Lee was arrested and a bond of $1,500 was announced, but she didn't have the money to be released and was put in a cell at the branch jail. She was eventually released through the charity of two known Bisbee men, B. Caretto and Fred Fuss, who paid her bond. When Hattie left jail, she went to the Palace Undertaking Company to visit Carson's body and wept over him.

Two days before the Carson shooting, a fire broke out at Lee's home. A series of explosions were caused by the combustion of gun cartridges stored in a back room. Witnesses said that at around 9:00 a.m. they heard gunshots coming from inside the woman's house. As neighbors ran to investigate, they saw Lee run toward Bisbee. She left as the flimsy wooden home was consumed by fire within minutes.

Neighbors reported that frequent domestic disturbances at Lee's house were a nuisance, and because of the bad reputation of its tenants, people suspected the fire may have been intentional in order to hide traces of a crime. People were so leery that a search of the burned ruins was initiated. Nothing was found, but neighbors thought a skeleton might pop up somewhere in the ashes. Their suspicion about the activities in the house was somewhat ominous. The controversial woman was not seen again until the day Carson was killed.

At Hattie Lee's preliminary hearing sometime after, she was put back in jail. Judge Grier stated that he thought her being charged with burning down her house and her threat to kill Mrs. McBride were reasons to believe she was guilty. So he sent her back to jail to await trial.

Lee had her next hearing with the same judge on June 5 and was now facing three felony charges instead of two. She was now specifically accused of attempting to defraud the National Fire Insurance Company of Hartford, Connecticut. She ended up having to pay two $1,000 fines, one for the defrauding charge and one for Mrs. McBride's complaint of threating to kill her. Miraculously, Lee came up with the money and was released.

Mrs. McBride was found not guilty of the charge against her by the same court in Lowell with a trial by jury. On December 7 in Tombstone and after several hours, the jury of Mr. McBride's trial returned with the verdict of not guilty. It was known that the sentiment of the community of Lowell was almost unanimously in favor of Mr. McBride.

CAFÉ KILLER ON MAIN STREET

Imagine the streets of Bisbee in 1913, when the mining town was bustling with people walking in throngs up and down the sidewalks of Main Street, enjoying an evening and maybe grabbing a bite after a night at the theater. In November of that year, this was reality, but something suddenly distorted the cheerful scene. Two people were shot and killed instantly in the crowded Maze Café by a jealous rival of one of the victims. John W. Hall was killed by Roy Haigler, who emptied his pistol while also mortally wounding a bystander from Douglas named Frank Hall and critically wounding a high school student named George Seeley. (There was never a mention in any source that the two Hall men were related.)

A large crowd of customers occupied the Maze Café's tables, lunch counter and booths. The café had a bar, which was also full. Frank Hall and the young Seeley were with other members of a car club from Douglas that had driven in a caravan to Bisbee. Their initial plan was to turn back around, but the men decided to eat first.

As Hall and Seeley went inside the café, they made their way to the stools and the lunch counter a little after 10:00 p.m. They had their backs to the booths and didn't notice Haigler and Anna Johnson sitting at one of them. The pair had arrived just a few moments before.

According to the article "Two Killed Instantly" in the *Bisbee Daily Review*, the shooting took place just minutes after members of the car club entered the building. Witnesses said that the first shot sounded like a loud crack and was followed by a second and then four more shots in rapid succession. As soon as the gun went off, customers rushed for the front door in full panic. As soon as they made it outside, they were met by a crush of men trying to get in after hearing the gunshots from the street.

As bullets began to fly in the direction of the Douglas men, they were stunned. They froze but then began to move toward the door. A club car member named Clarence Hinton was sitting next to Frank Hall, but as soon as the gunfire erupted, he turned to Seeley, who was on his right side and nearest to the door.

Hinton told Seeley that they should get out of there. The teenager murmured: "I can't. I'm shot." Hinton wrapped his arms around Seeley and, without looking around for his other friends, ran with Seeley into the street. He was focused on the wounded boy and didn't notice Frank Hall on the floor, dead. Hinton later said that Frank was sitting on the far end of the counter, and Hinton figured he could fend for himself and get out too.

Just a few minutes after the shooting, Deputy Sheriff Red Gannon rushed into the café. Haigler saw him and confessed to the shooting and was arrested without resistance. He was immediately taken to the County Branch Jail on OK Street.

The café owner, John Hart, was in an adjoining booth to Johnson and Haigler's when the shots were fired. He said that John Hall was in his bar a few minutes before the incident. John returned rather quickly. Hart said that when the gunfire started, he turned his back into the other direction and heard John Hall gasp: "My God! He has shot me."

The Douglas teen was carried to the office of Dr. Hawley in the Allen Block on Subway Street. The doctor administered first aid, and the patient was taken to the Copper Queen Hospital, where surgeons discovered that a bullet had gone through the meaty part of his thigh. He was expected to make a full recovery. The bodies of the dead men were taken to the Palace Undertaking Company up the street.

Johnson stated to the newspaper that she and Haigler were sitting in a booth at the Maze Café enjoying a light meal when John W. Hall appeared in the doorway. It was thought that the man had followed them there. She said Haigler started to shoot as soon as he saw Hall. The twenty-one-year-old woman said that John W. Hall had threatened her and that he would shoot her if he ever caught her and Haigler together.

In the jail cell that night, Haigler told a reporter from the *Review* that he and Miss Johnson were sitting in a booth when John W. Hall appeared. He stated: "Hall came to the booth and apparently reached for his gun. When I saw his action I pulled my revolver, got it out first and began shooting." He added: "That is all I have got to say. Miss Johnson is a friend of mine. I had never met Hall but had seen him often."

Haigler had no idea he had shot and killed a second person and wounded another until after he was arrested. When he learned of the full extent of the catastrophe, he was very sorry for Frank Hall's death and for injuring Seeley.

During Haigler's preliminary trial for the murders some weeks later, Johnson testified that she had kept company with John W. Hall for over three years and only met the shooter six months prior. She said she had become very close with Haigler and that Hall grew jealous and at different times threatened to kill her and Haigler if she kept seeing him.

The young woman confirmed several letters she had written to Haigler; these were presented in court. In these letters she warned him of John Hall's threats. During cross-examination, she was asked about her relationship with Haigler. The defense attorney objected, as this would only discredit her reputation and degrade her. That was sustained.

Three witnesses testified that they saw a fistfight between Haigler and John W. Hall about three months before. The owner of the Maze Café, Mr. Hart, also testified and was asked if he made the statement that he saw Haigler point his gun at Johnson. He denied saying it, but W.C.T. Todd, a reporter, testified to hearing Hart make that statement. The newspaper article Todd wrote including that remark was introduced into evidence by the defense.

Haigler repeated his narrative on the stand that John W. Hall had gone for his gun first and that, because of the many threats Hall had made to Johnson before, Haigler pulled out his gun and shot in self-defense. After the court proceedings, Haigler was taken back to the County Branch Jail.

Haigler was still in confinement in January and was charged with murder in the first degree. He originally had his lawyer, William Cleary, request a bond to be set, but Superior Court Judge Lockwood ruled against it. At the time, there had been no standard established in Arizona for interpreting the language of the statute governing the right of a defendant to be given bail when charged with murder in the first degree. Judge Lockwood wanted the Arizona Supreme Court to accept the application for bail on a writ of habeas corpus. It did.

Eventually, Haigler's bond was set at $10,000. District Attorney W.G. Gilmore agreed with that amount but would rather it be higher. On March 28, Haigler was released, and his trial was finally set for April 20 of the same year. The trial lasted just over a week. The jury deliberated for twenty minutes and brought back a verdict of acquittal. The thought was that this decision was credited to Johnson's testimony, as she now swore she saw John W. Hall reach as if to draw his gun on Haigler. This matched Haigler's testimony of self-defense. Charges for the death of Frank Hall and the injury to Seeley were never brought against Haigler after the trail.

Dead Man Phones Police

A prominent Bisbee man called police on February 25, 1913, to report his own death. Seconds later, it was true. Jim Cresto, thirty-eight, shot himself in the head. This was reported by the *Bisbee Daily Review*. His wife tried to stop him, but his determination was too strong for her. At 2:15 p.m., a phone call came to the police station, and Officer Parley McRae answered. The voice on the other end said: "This is Jim Cresto. Come up here and get me. I'm dead."

McRae stated that after Cresto stopped speaking he could hear a terrorizing scream and some kind of short scuffle. The officer dropped the phone immediately and ran to Cresto's house, located on the hill between Temby Avenue and Opera Drive.

By the time Officer McRae arrived, a small crowd had formed in front of the house. The officer walked into the home and saw the body of Cresto half lying on the floor and half leaning against a sewing machine. The dead man had a bullet wound to the right ear, and blood was splattered on the phone receiver, which was still swinging.

The Bisbee policeman stated in the article that he had known Cresto for many years and that the moment he got the call he made a run for Cresto's house. He said, "The sound of a scuffle was caused by his wife trying to hold his hand, in which he held a revolver, while talking to me." To be exact, the weapon Cresto used was a .41-caliber gun mounted on a .45-caliber frame. According to reports, the bullet entered the right ear, traveled up and entered his brain. His death was instant.

McRae added, "From the position of the body, Cresto holding the receiver with his left hand, shoved his wife away and still standing at the telephone, put the gun to his right ear and fired."

A postcard of a view of Bisbee from Quality Hill. *Author's collection.*

Cresto was a popular man in town. An immigrant from Italy, he had lived in Bisbee for fifteen years at the time of his demise. The day before his death, he was seen at a close friend's funeral and seemed despondent afterward. Almost a week before the funeral, he had asked a friend to borrow a gun to go hunting. The friend said no.

On the afternoon of his suicide, Cresto had been working at his small lunch stand in Brewery Gulch. He went home to eat. His wife had his meal on the table. According to his wife, he had been feeling a little down for several days, but on that day, he seemed like his usual self. It was not until she heard him on the phone that she knew he was quite the opposite.

He left behind his wife and two children.

HUSBAND'S FAILED SUICIDE ATTEMPT

A man experienced a grief so tremendous that he tried to end his life, but failed. William White lived in a neighborhood near the Johnson Addition in the area known as Jiggerville. The area was named for the mine bosses ("jiggers") who lived there. White was found by a neighbor at his house at 3:00 p.m. about an hour and a half after he tried to end his life with a hefty amount of chloroform. White's wife had died during a trip to visit her mother in Dallas, Texas, several weeks before.

A local newspaper reported that a full bottle of chloroform was found on the bed near White and a poison-saturated handkerchief was over his face when his neighbor came by to check on him. White had taken a swallow of the chloroform and then laid the wet cloth on his mouth. A lot of the chloroform was still in the bottle, enough to kill him. The amount he had ingested and what he inhaled from the handkerchief was enough only to knock him out. That prevented White from drinking more and completing his mission. A pistol was found under his pillow.

The widower left a letter for the neighbor in which he said goodbye to his friends. He wrote that the grief over the death of his wife was too much. White was sent to the Copper Queen Hospital and fully recovered.

4

THE BISBEE MINER

*W*hen the Bisbee District was booming, men from all parts of the country and the world came looking for a job or a claim strike. They came from Germany, Mexico, Poland, England, Italy, Serbia and Ireland. The average pay for a Bisbee miner at its early stages was about $3.50 a day. By 1920, it was $6.00 an hour. The median hourly pay for an underground copper miner as of January 2023 is $25.25.

Bisbee's population has fluctuated during its existence, from around 1,700 in 1890 to its highest, 20,000. Miners were the heart of the town and worked extremely hard under dangerous conditions. They relied on brute strength and used steel and dynamite as their tools. Hundreds of miners were underground per shift. A Bisbee miner would start his shift by changing from his street clothes to his "diggers." Clothes were encrusted with dirt and sweat from the previous day. The miners would hang those clothes on a hook or place them in a basket in the changing room.

The miner would next "brass in" for his shift. He went to the wall of identification tags and got one from the timekeeper. When his shift was done, he gave it back to be hung in its rightful place. This verified that the miner was back on the surface and safe.

One of the underground operation positions was the "mucker." This person shoveled broken ore into a car, then pushed it to a designated area, where it was brought to the surface. The "driller" was a miner who pierced holes in the rock for dynamite and blasting. With the coming of

Bisbee miners, 1913. These men played as hard as they worked and were a testimony to their own strength and bravery during an era when the mining industry's policies and safety were in their primitive stages. *Author's collection.*

the industrial era, the miners' work was made easier. A miner drilling by hand would get through inches in a day; a drill machine's progress was measured by the foot.

Although the new machine was faster, the air-driven drill was nicknamed the "Widowmaker." A piston was operated by compressed air that hammered into the mountain as it rotated the drill chuck. Because water was not used for lubrication, a large amount of dust was created in the process. The dust would get into the driller's lungs and caused silicosis. The silicon dioxide dust would evolve into fragments that caused scarring in the lungs. After just a year or two of drilling, a miner would be too ill to work and typically died within six months.

The miners were a tight-knit group; once they were underground, they became a brotherhood. This meant they played as hard as they worked. The shaft elevator or cage was a great way to introduce new employees into that exclusive club. It was used in a roguish way and as a tool of "initiation" for new miners.

On a miner's very first shift, the "cager" would be notified when he boarded and would flip the switch to lower at a very high speed. He then would suddenly stop the cage in midflight, bringing the "sardine-packed" elevator to a hard jerk and everyone to their knees. The new miner would be filled with fear as his coworkers roared with laughter.

THE BISBEE DEPORTATION OF 1917

The infamous Bisbee Deportation was an incredible and mind-blowing event that took place in 1917. This event involved kidnapping and the incarceration of miners and town citizens. The IWW had a strong presence

Deportation train being loaded by armed men. *Author's collection.*

in Arizona at the time. It was active in promoting equal rights for minorities and safety in the workplace. The IWW presented a list of demands to the Bisbee mining company. As a result of that, the Bisbee Miners Union called a strike on June 24, and by the twenty-seventh, half of the Bisbee workforce had followed suit. The IWW, or "Wobblies," also had a reputation for exhibiting bad behavior to justify their strikes and to deter miners from going back to work.

The Wobblies were said to be connected to aggressive and intimidating crimes in Bisbee over a course of about three weeks. Because of that, Harry C. Wheeler, Arizona Ranger captain and at the time Cochise County sheriff who made his temporary headquarters in Bisbee, wrote an open letter that was printed in the *Bisbee Review* on July 12, 1917.

In the letter, he warned all women and children to keep off the streets that day. He said he had formed a sheriff's posse of 1,200 men in Bisbee and 1,000 in Douglas. He wrote that they were all loyal Americans and had been deputized the day before or that morning.

He stated that he formed the posse for the purpose of arresting people on charges of vagrancy, treason or disturbing the peace. He said that in all areas of Bisbee, including Lowell and the Warren District, men who were working or wanted to go back to work were being harassed, threatened and insulted. The mayor had also been threatened. There were threats to destroy the homes of those who were working, and men were reported to have been assaulted and brutally beaten.

He ended the letter with these words:

> *All arrested persons will be treated humanely, and their cases examined with justice and care. I hope no resistance will be made, for I desire no bloodshed. However, I am determined if resistance is made, it shall be quickly and effectively overcome.*
> —*Harry C. Wheeler, Sheriff Cochise County, Arizona*

Warning posters were placed everywhere in Cochise County. They warned that the Citizen's Protective Association and the Workmen's Loyalty League were determined to make the Warren District unhealthy for Wobblies and their supporters. These people were warned to keep away from the Warren District. Mayor Jacob Erickson closed City Park the night before the deportation, as this was their meeting place.

The morning of July 12 began at daylight for the IWW members. The first thing on their schedule was to get on the picket lines. By 6:30 a.m., the streets and alleys of Bisbee were bursting with heavily armed citizens. The post office was a favorite gathering place during the strike for IWW protestors. In an article in the *Bisbee Daily Review*, "1200 I.W.W. Deported from District by Citizens," it was reported, "Like rabbits from their burrows, the 'Wobblies' began emerging at daylight…sensed nothing of the impending disaster to their cause."

As the Wobblies blissfully continued with their daily protesting, a whistle blew from an unidentified person's lips. Instantly, an armed man mysteriously emerged from the post office; another came out from the alley in the rear of the building; and another jumped from the alley from the Subway. The Wobblies were surrounded. They instantly stood at attention and then threw up their hands without any objection.

They were searched for guns, but none were confiscated. From then until 7:30 a.m., the strikers were gathered from every part of Bisbee. The deputized men searched for strikers, known advocates of the Wobblies and anyone who couldn't account for themselves. They looked in rooming houses, hotels, private houses, the union hall on OK Street and every possible hiding place one could imagine. A few miners were handled with not much aggression, while others were forced at gunpoint to leave their homes. Men between the ages of twenty-one and thirty, Bisbee business men, property owners, husbands, fathers, sons and brothers were all being gathered. Most of them were brought in front of the post office, and when a large enough number was gathered, Sheriff Wheeler gave the order for the men to march.

The procession passed down Subway Street to the depot plaza, then crossed the streetcar tracks and then followed the train tracks of the El Paso and Southwestern to Lowell. As they walked, there was an armed guard on either of their sides. Men who were just getting off shift from the mine ran home and grabbed their guns and joined the procession.

It was reported that in some places of the line, it was ten men across, blocking any cars and pedestrians heading toward Lowell. The distance was approximately three miles, and along the parade route, they were held at gunpoint by deputies in cars carrying machine guns.

A call for assistance was made to Douglas, where a staggering three hundred armed men from the smelter answered the call and drove to Bisbee. They parked in Lowell and jumped right into the procession. More marchers were added as they made their way to the entrance of the Warren neighborhood.

The procession moved south toward Warren Ball Park. They entered the park and poured through the open northwest gate. They filled up the grandstand and overflowed to the baseball diamond. The armed guards surrounded the entire park as more men flooded into the stadium.

A freight engine pulling twenty-three cars arrived with its whistle blowing at 11:00 a.m. The men were forced to walk through a long line of armed

Deportation march from Bisbee to Warren. *Author's collection.*

Another view of strikers being loaded into train cars. *Author's collection.*

men, some pointing their guns at them. They were asked whether they were willing to go back to work. Those who chose to work were hustled out of the area as the order to load the Wobblies was given. The men who refused were lined up 40 to 50 at a time and were put on the train. It took almost one hour to load twenty-four train cars with the approximately 1,200 men to be hauled to Columbus, New Mexico. Armed guards were placed on top of the cars. A warning whistle was blown, and the prisoners were hauled out of Bisbee.

I must mention that several men were saved by family from the deportation. When a guard was flagged down by a relative, a quick conversation was made regarding if a captured man was meritorious. If he was found to be so, he was pulled from a loading line. Witnesses reported that there were also several wives who walked or ran along the side of the train cursing Bisbee, its people and everything within.

The train headed toward Douglas and stopped at Lee Station, ten miles east, where train crews were changed and water barrels placed in cars. The train was guarded by about two hundred armed Douglas citizens, and machine guns were manned on two small hills along the way.

At the smelting plants of the Copper Queen branch of the Phelps-Dodge Corporation and the Calumet and Arizona Company, guards were posted to safeguard the buildings.

The train arrived at Columbus, New Mexico, between 9:30 p.m. and 10:00 p.m. that night. They left Columbus around midnight and arrived at a place called Hermanas at 3:00 a.m. It was reported that the train cars were overcrowded and a lot of men had to stand for the duration of the trip. When the train stopped, the deported men realized they were left unguarded and were left with water but no food. They also concluded they were now in Hermanas.

They were at a government-maintained camp for the deportees in New Mexico and at the same site of the Mexican and Chinese refugee camp that General Pershing established on the "plains of death" between Columbus and the International line.

According to another article in the *Bisbee Daily Review*, "Deported Men Army Guests at Columbus," a tent city was organized for the miners. They were returned by an escort from Columbus by the United States Cavalry. The entire camp was under guard by soldiers with sidearms with no one being permitted to enter the camp without a pass.

The deported men had to set up their own tents, dig pits for field kitchens, haul firewood and construct sinking latrines. They were given canned beef, canned tomatoes and bread with a ration of coffee. During their imprisonment, water was hauled by the cavalry from a railroad water tank somewhat nearby. If it rained, they had to use the train cars as shelter.

Train leaving Warren Ballpark in the distance while family and friends look on. *Author's collection.*

W.B. Cleary, a Bisbee attorney and labor advocate, was one of the men who was put on the train to New Mexico that hot July day. He took unofficial charge of the deported men at the camp and made a statement to the press. He said that an exact number of 1,286 men were deported from Bisbee and, with a few exceptions, were all underground miners. He said the men were on strike for better conditions, particularly for two men to be on a machine, which is the norm for most mining companies. Cleary also stated that the miners wanted the mandatory physical exams to end as a part of the hiring process. The complaint was that when they didn't pass for whatever reason, they would be blacklisted.

The other demands made by the miners were to discontinue all blasting during the shift and for two men to work together in all rises. They also demanded the abolition of all bonus and contract work and the abolishment of the sliding scale and for all underground miners to have a flat rate of $6.00 per shift, with the surface workers to have $5.50. The last of the demands was for there to be no discrimination against members based on their political affiliations and principles.

It was also reported that the Bisbee police records showed far fewer arrests during the time of the strike than when they weren't striking. The strikers were members of an assortment of organizations, including the Mill and Smelter Workers' Union, members of the IWW and the International Mine.

Incredibly, the only recorded occurrences during the deportation were the shootings of O.P. McRae and James Brew. McRae was a miner who was deputized and heading a search party. He started toward a house in Jiggerville. The area was located near Lowell. He did not see or know that Brew lived there.

Brew looked out through a screen door from his house and, when he spotted McRae walking up his steps, fired three fatal shots at him. McRae almost died instantly, being hit high on the right side of his chest.

Brew ran through the house and out the back door and around the premises. As he turned around the side of his house, one of the deputies shot him in his chest. Brew had been a member of the Wobblies,

McRae was thirty-three and from St. David and worked for the Calumet & Arizona Company for ten years. He left behind a wife and three children. He had four brothers and two sisters. It was said that McRae was one of the best-known men in the Warren District and was one of the best-liked employees.

MANY OPINIONS REGARDING THIS event were reported in newspapers across the nation. Some supported Sherriff Wheeler and the mining company's actions, while others condemned them. Members of the Associated Press were invited to cover the activities at the encampment and found that the men made a formal offer for Cleary to organize a regiment with him as their leader. They wanted to immediately leave for the trenches of the theater of war in Europe at the time. They did not want to be known as slackers and were willing to fight for their principles. The entire population of the camp was reported to follow all orders of the camp.

Finally, an appointed mediator from the Department of Labor for Arizona sent a direct message to President Woodrow Wilson regarding the deportation. The message was signed by Arizona governor G.W.P. Hunt and Arizona judge John McBride. The president ordered an investigation of the incident. Eventually, it was found that no federal law applied. It was referred to the State of Arizona that such events be made criminal by federal statute. They found the mining company was at fault and boosted the efforts of the IWW.

CALAMITIES

Reports in the local paper were not scarce regarding miners being injured in an assortment of accidents and underground situations. In 1910, Bisbee miner, Frank Huckleby was crushed by a cage. He was severely injured with three broken ribs and a broken leg, with several lacerations on his head.

The Holbrook Mine in Bisbee was a popular site for accidents and where the underground operations were intense and where the miners worked fast. In 1904, Jack O'Neil was injured in the mine, and he died. He was bent over an ore car when a cave-in happened. A rock crushed his ribs. He was quickly found and removed and taken to the Copper Queen Hospital. They tried to save him, but his injuries were too serious. He had six broken ribs, all of which had penetrated his lungs. The accident happened at 2:00 p.m.; O'Neil died at 6:20 p.m.

In 1908, a thirty-five-year-old miner named John Wood was working in that same mine. His leg got caught between the cage and the shaft timbering. His injuries were so severe that he had to have his leg amputated.

It seemed that mining accidents happened in threes, and miners believed in the Hoodoo superstition. In 1903, three men working in the Holbrook shaft were hurt in three separate accidents. Immediately following a dynamite blast, a piece of the mountain fell on H.L. Fenner. This broke his shoulder and pinned him to the ground. Martin Eiting was severely injured by another explosion in an old hole in a different location of the shaft. He was wounded in the chest and arms. The third accident involved Reuben Davidson, who fell thirty feet from a ladder and injured his back.

The intensity of danger in the underground tunnels may have caused the miners to experience high levels of stress and anxiety. So much that Steve Cole dreamt of his death the night before he died. In 1911, Cole was working for the Copper Queen Company and was injured in the Southwestern slope properties area. The well-known miner had been on their payroll for about five years at that point.

On a December morning, he and another worker went to the new slope to do some timbering. A boulder fell on Cole and crushed his leg and pinned him to the ground. A group of miners tried to extricate him. Cole never lost consciousness, and his mind was clear. He directed the miners throughout the ordeal. The way the rock was positioned, if they tried to roll it, the boulder might move onto his body. The injured man instructed them how to pry it off.

On his way to the Copper Queen Hospital, still conscious, he told his friends to make sure his leg was not amputated. It was horribly crushed, and he had bled severely. He also told them about his dream. One of his coworkers said the man dreamt that he would be killed in the mine that day and, when he began his shift, stopped and started to leave to go home. Unfortunately, he decided to ignore his vision and ended up paying for it.

His friends expected him to recover, as his injury didn't seem fatal. Evidently, with the loss of that much blood and the amount of pain he suffered, Cole went into a state of shock and died that afternoon.

Forty-three-year-old miner Frank Balma was a Bisbee resident for twenty-five years and met his death in the Junction Mine in the spring of 1911. When a boulder crushed him, he instantly died. He left a wife and three children.

Accidents weren't the sole reason why miners were killed underground. Joe Picklick was hit on the head with a piece of iron pipe on the four-hundred-foot level of the Czar Mine in 1918. A miner named Frank Velard was his killer. Picklick's skull was fractured, and he was in and out of consciousness most of the time before his death. His death certificate states that he died on December 7 and the cause was a fractured skull. Picklick was thirty-one years old and was an immigrant from Poland.

Even the most experienced miner might have a bad day, as did William M. Evans in 1904. He and his son Seth were working at the Red Jacket and Bisbee Mine. Because of Evan's carelessness, an uncharted explosion took place.

The father and son were approximately 160 feet underground at the bottom of the shaft. They were preparing to charge the drill holes. They were forewarned that there was dynamite powder in those holes. Even so, William Evans decided to use a scrap-metal pole to push down the charge into one of those holes. That didn't work, so he took his hammer and began to hit it. He swung his hammer just once or twice when the charge exploded.

Evans's left hand was completely blown from his wrist. He was thrown into the air, as was his son, who was at his side when it happened. Seth was severely bruised on his legs and body but had no serious injuries.

As soon as the explosion happened, the emergency alarm sounded, and Stewart Hunt, the mine's superintendent, was called. He in turn called a doctor who was nearby. The doctor quickly arrived and addressed the wound of William Evans. He and his son were transferred to the Calumet and Arizona Hospital, where William was operated on. His hand was completely severed, and because of a ragged tear of flesh, the doctor had to amputate further onto the wrist for a cleaner and healthier cut.

Mr. Evans was an older and respected miner who was thought of as a competent man. When he was asked why he had been so foolish as to try to drill the powdered hole even after he had been warned of the danger, he replied that "he blamed no person but himself and that he could give no reason for having done so."

Another miner, William Wright, was killed on the eight-hundred-foot level in the Spray Mine in 1906. At approximately 9:00 p.m., one hundred tons of ore and dirt buried Wright. Without warning, a cave-in took place. A half dozen or more men working nearby saw it happen but fortunately were out of range of the falling debris.

The miners gave the alarm, and with more help they began to dig Wright out. It took about a half hour for them to recover his body. It was thought that as soon as he was pummeled with that much weight he died instantly. The opinion was that his heart was pierced by ribs on the left side that had been crushed into his body.

A terrible mining accident that may have ever been recorded in Bisbee included three miners who were mangled and suffered powder burns. The incident took place in the Pittsburg and Duluth shaft in February 1904. Frank Hollister, Mike Mollander and Dominick Docesco were at the bottom of the shaft. They had just finished taking down the powder to charge the dynamite holes for blasting. The men placed the powder on the ground and set it by their sides and began to prepare to fill the drilled holes. No one knew how, but the powder somehow was ignited and set fire to the clothing of the three men. They tried to signal for help, but the engineer on shift didn't hear them. He knew something was wrong and realized an accident had occurred because of the smoke. Soon more smoke and fumes were detected. A group of men decided to investigate and went to a cage and were lowered to a scene of horror.

The three injured men were lying on the rocks at the bottom of the shaft. Mollander and Docesco were taken up first, alive and severely burned. Their flesh was burnt, black and crisp. Another half an hour passed before they retrieved Hollister's body to the surface. His head was split open, the flesh hung from his body in ribbons and fell off like burnt paper crumbling at the touch. He was dead; Mollander died the next day.

In 1922, two men were injured in the Sacramento Mine. William Jowles broke both of his legs and Grady L. Dungan hurt his back. The men were working in a drift and for some unapparent reason an ore car overturned on them, trapping them underneath. They were taken to the Copper Queen Hospital and recovered.

Not only miners succumbed in the Bisbee tunnels, but also members of the company's administration. Charles Warner was the assistant superintendent of mines for the Copper Queen Company and in 1904 was fatally injured in the Holbrook Mine. His accident took place between the three-hundred- and four-hundred-foot-level. Apparently, he was ill with pleurisy, which causes sharp chest pain that worsens during breathing. It was reported that for several days he had severe pains in his chest, which caused him choking sensations, dizziness and fainting spells. When he suffered those sharp pains, he would lean against a wall or anything that could support him.

Witnesses said that Warner had planned to get off at the four-hundred level. When the cage reached the three-hundred level, it looked like he was stepping forward, as if to get off. Instead of stepping off the cage, he fell while it was still in motion, and his body was caught between the hood and side plates. It was thought that he may have fainted while the cage was in motion. The cage dropped very fast, and as soon as it reached the four-hundred level, it stopped. Warner was taken out and brought to the surface.

He was taken to the Copper Queen Hospital, where doctors found he had a fractured skull. The fracture extended clear around his head. Warner died and two days later was celebrated with a long procession of family and friends at his elaborate funeral.

Bisbee funeral, circa 1898, arranged by Hubbard's Mortuary. This somber scene was sadly a frequent event in Bisbee's notorious years. *Courtesy Bisbee Mining & Historical Museum, Opie Burgess Collection.*

His remains were taken from the Palace Undertaking Parlor to the Masonic Hall with pallbearers who were all members of the Masonic Order. During his funeral services, the streets of Bisbee were full of men and their wives of the several fraternities of which he was a member. There was a choir during the memorial ceremony, and over one hundred miners who had worked for Warner walked in the funeral procession. Everyone walked behind a wagon hearse that was pulled by sable-black horses with pallbearers marching slowly beside it. A carriage occupied by the family was behind, as well as carriages of other members of the family and friends. Witnesses reported that there was a string of 175 carriages in all. That afternoon, almost every place in Bisbee, including the Copper Queen Mine, was closed in honor of Warner. It was a true tribute for the Bisbee miner.

The last phrase from the 1918 poem "Miners" by Wilfred Owen is as follows:

> *The centuries will burn rich loads; With which we groaned; Whose warmth shall lull their dreaming lids; While songs are crooned; But they will not dream of us poor lads; Left in the ground.*

5

BREWERY GULCH

here is a section of Bisbee that has glowed in the spectra of what we might think of as the Wild West. Brewery Gulch was originally tagged as the "Hottest Spot between St. Louis and San Francisco" in its prime, which would be around the early 1900s. Brewery Gulch is where Main Street turns into Naco Road. At this location, the Dubacher brothers opened a drinkery. They built the Mountain Brewery, which became a popular place not only where local miners hung out, but also travelers took a rest and had a cold drink. This is where Brewery Gulch derived its name and where the brothers' nephew Joseph Muheim started to work in Bisbee, as a bartender.

Their saloon was named the "best equipped establishment of its kind in the territory of Arizona." Among the infamous rascals who patronized the brewery were Burt Alvord, Billy Stiles and "Black Jack." Brewery Gulch grew along with the rest of the mining community. This business district was packed with approximately forty-seven saloons at one time. The number of actual saloons varies in historical documents.

A handful of factors may be the reason the "Gulch" was thick with a variety of recreational businesses for decades. The sole miner who would most likely be passing through, was single with no children and a hole burning in his pocket, to blow money on whiskey and women in the tenderloin. I cover Bisbee prostitution in the next chapter.

The saloon doors up and down Brewery Gulch never closed; the businesses were open twenty-four hours a day to oblige the miner who would walk in

Left: Bustling Brewery Gulch was always packed, mostly with men tending to a variety of businesses. But it was also known to have reputable women and their children shop at a variety of markets and have lunch at one of its several cafés. *Author's collection.*

Below: A bird's-eye view of the entry at Brewery Gulch with the line of buildings curving Brewery Avenue. These are now gone. In the background and to the left are houses on Chihuahua Hill. Straight back are homes at Upper Brewery Gulch. *Author's collection.*

after one of the three shifts, day or night. The clatter of men drinking until they were completely smashed and letting their tempers get the best of them, resulting in brawls, would make Wyatt Earp shake his head in shock. This type of activity existed alongside civility. The entry of Brewery Gulch was packed with meat markets, suitable restaurants, a very large theater called the Orpheum and barbershops. It was an area of the Gulch where women could bring their children and meet friends. It was bustling with people, horses and wagons and later with the automobile.

It survived the Prohibition era masterfully, as some of the saloons were turned into soft-drink fountains or had underground tunnels that led to several speakeasy bars or stored large stocks of different types of alcohol. Entertainment from musicals, serious theater, movies and gambling were all part of the colorful environment of what locals, with endearment, referred to as the Gulch. It is still the most popular area in Bisbee to let off steam and let loose. In recent decades and to present times, the streets are filled with events. From bikers to buskers and pet parades, Brewery Gulch is still living as a notorious place filled with the Wild West spirit.

Saloons Galore

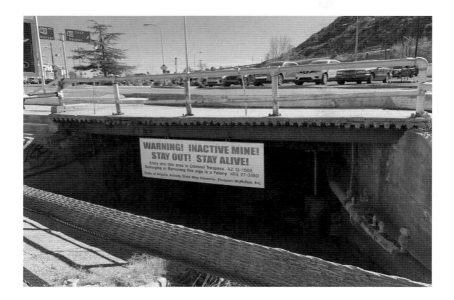

Opposite: Brewery Gulch's entry. There is a clear warning from the Freeport-McMoRan and Gold Mining Company at an entry to one of the many tunnels under the streets of Bisbee. *Author's collection.*

Left: Brewery Gulch and the staggering amount of signage displaying its many businesses when the street was still not yet paved. *Author's collection.*

Below: Brewery Gulch plaque. *Author's collection.*

A look at the houses above Brewery Avenue. These have existed for over one hundred years and characterize a period of Bisbee's fascinating past. *Author's collection*.

THE BREWERY GULCH RACE RIOT OF 1919

The day before a large Fourth of July parade was to take place in the town of Bisbee in 1919, a shocking event occurred involving the Buffalo Soldiers of the Tenth Cavalry and the city's police. This is known as the Brewery Gulch Race Riot and is a page of Bisbee's history that marks a grim era of the times. Many people were wounded, including Black soldiers, a deputy sheriff and a woman who was shot in the head. At the time of the riot, the officers from the Tenth Cavalry were at a dance given in their honor in Warren, about three miles south of Brewery Gulch.

According to an article in the *Bisbee Daily Review*, on the night of July 3, the trouble began in front of the Silver Leaf Club, segregated for Black individuals and located at Upper Brewery Gulch. Around 9:30 or 10:00 p.m., a group of five Black soldiers were standing outside the club. George Sullivan, who was out of Douglas and was an on-duty military policeman (MP) of the Nineteenth U.S. Infantry, walked past the club. As he passed the group of men, he and witnesses reported that the soldiers, who were intoxicated, spouted rude remarks and taunted him. Sullivan said he realized they were drunk and told them they had better go home.

As soon as that was said, the group of men drew their guns and jumped Sullivan, knocking him to the ground. During the scuffle, they grabbed his revolver from him. People in the streets quickly came to Sullivan's rescue and tore the men away. The soldiers released the man and ran directly to the Bisbee police station.

They reported to Chief Kempton that "civilians were trying to run them out of town." The chief told them they should leave their guns at the station. The soldiers refused and told him they were permitted by their officers to carry them, and they left the station still armed. (According to reports, Colonel White, who was their commander, said that the weapons they were carrying were part of their army-issued equipment. They were carrying sidearms and ammunition under U.S. regulations for the tactical march they would be performing in the next day's Fourth of July Parade.)

Kempton, Officer William Sherill and Deputy Sheriff Joseph B. Hardwick took to Brewery Gulch and began to search for all Black soldiers in the area to disarm them, as they suspected that trouble was coming.

As soon as the lawmen approached the Silver Leaf Club, five other soldiers came out of the building, shooting their firearms. One bullet hit Hardwick in the arm, leaving a flesh wound. As random bullets struck a brick wall, the dust clouded the eyes of the officers. They emptied their

Top: Buffalo Soldiers, Nineteenth Cavalry Drum Corps. *Author's collection.*

Bottom: The Bisbee Train Depot in 1905. During the shootout, the lawmen and soldiers would have been on the other side of the building. *Author's collection.*

guns into the powdered cloud. Officer Sherill's last shot struck one of the soldiers in the back of the neck, and the man fell hard to the ground.

The three lawmen ran back to the police station for more guns and ammo. The station was just around the corner from Brewery Gulch. As they rushed out the front entrance of the station, they saw a car with several Black soldiers and commanded them to stop. The driver hit the brakes in front of the train depot located across the street and opened fire on the officers. Deputy Hardwick and Officer Sherrill shot back and shattered the car's windows. One of the bullets ricocheted and hit a nineteen-year-old Bisbee woman named Teresa Leyvas in the right side of her head. She was waiting at the depot for a train at the time. Doctors who attended to her gunshot wound said that it was not dangerous, and the bullet was easily extracted from her scalp.

The men in the car surrendered with their hands up right after the lawmen returned gun fire. They were immediately arrested and sent to jail. Lieutenant F.H. Ryden of the Tenth Cavalry went with Chief Kempton to the Silver Leaf Club to persuade the remaining soldiers to return in military formation to the camp at Warren. Kempton promised them security on their march, which was a two- to three-mile hike. The men agreed, then Lieutenant Ryder put them into march formation.

Two police cars followed behind the soldiers, but a small group began to fall back. They eventually fell so far behind that they lined themselves up with the police cars and began to argue with the lawmen. Then they decided to run away. One soldier made it up to Brewery Avenue and decided to hide behind a telephone pole at an entrance of City Park. He was very drunk and wasn't in a good mindset. He reached for his gun and pointed it to shoot, but Deputy Hardwick saw him and opened fire instantly. The deputy managed to shoot the soldier in the right side of his chest, and the bullet penetrated the man's lung. The wounded man slid to the ground, unconscious, and was taken to the hospital. The other soldiers were caught shortly after, and their guns were confiscated.

Because most of the Black regiment of the Tenth Cavalry were now indisposed, two troops from the First Cavalry were ordered to Bisbee. Those in authority had not yet made the decision to allow the Black soldiers to march in the parade. The men from the First Cavalry were in Douglas and had to scramble to make the roughly twenty-nine mile trip to Bisbee by morning.

It was also reported that more than one hundred gunshots were fired during the riot and forty-one soldiers were arrested and disarmed. By midnight, the soldiers had turned themselves over to the officers of the Tenth Cavalry, who had to leave the dance at the Warren Country Club. In all, eight hundred Black soldiers were under the command of Colonel George B. White from Fort Huachuca. Three hundred of the soldiers were in Bisbee when the riot began, with the remaining five hundred back at camp.

The *Arizona Republican* reported that the Black regiment did indeed participate in the parade, along with six hundred soldiers of the First Cavalry and several Bisbee organizations. The newspaper stated that the town was thick with MPs and local lawmen.

The riot was documented as being caused by an irresponsible few who fell under foolish influences. That this was out of the ordinary and is not typical

U.S. Army troops marching in a similar parade in Lowell as to how they did on the Fourth of July 1919 on Main Street in Bisbee. *Author's collection.*

of the relationship between Fort Huachuca and Bisbee. Soldiers stated that they would continue cordial relations between the mining town and Fort Huachuca.

St. Elmo

The St. Elmo Bar, located in Brewery Gulch, has been in business since 1902, making this watering hole the oldest bar in Bisbee. The Palace Saloon in Prescott is the oldest frontier saloon in Arizona, having been established in 1877. This is when the town of Prescott was the Arizona Territory capital. The Palace was destroyed during the Whiskey Row fire in the summer of 1900, and a new building was put in its place the following year, causing the saloon to close for a period. Thus, St. Elmo has the title for longest continuously running bar in Arizona.

St. Elmo's first location was on Main Street directly next door to the original firehouse in Bisbee. It opened on March 10, 1902, under the management of Kleiner and Fawcett. The men had been in the saloon business in El Paso, Texas, and San Francisco, California, and had a good reputation in that line of commerce. In an announcement of the opening in the local newspaper, the owners stated that they planned to have gambling games and would always keep a good stock.

An announcement was made on February 28, 1906, that the Copper Queen Mining Company was going to add fifty thousand square feet to its store. This addition to Main Street brought about a new plan to erect bigger and better buildings around the same location. The Bank of Bisbee plans called for the building to be right across the alley on the same side of the street as St. Elmo. The new bank would be constructed in the location where the original firehouse was built.

Plans were also in progress for three men, M.J. Cunningham, William Robinson and Pete Johnson, to construct a two-story brick building on the present site of the saloon. The men were the owners of the land. The St. Elmo building was to be replaced by the new buildings by the summer of 1906. By April 10 of that year, the owners of St. Elmo were promised a rebate on their business license if they couldn't finish out for the full three months left on it. They had to vacate the building by the middle of the month, as construction would begin.

Luckily, a bartender at the saloon named William "Billy" Wolf, who also worked for the city, had plans of his own regarding the future of St. Elmo. In a newspaper announcement on April 28, 1906, it was reported that he had bought another business, the White House Saloon, located down on Brewery Gulch, from A.J. Bennett. He was relocating the saloon and bought all the fixtures from St. Elmo and installed them in the new location on the Gulch. By May 2, C.E. Rinehart had announced they were traveling back east to purchase the stock for his new drugstore, which would be in the future building.

As the old adobe structure had been torn down by May, John Smith, a Bisbee pioneer, recounted its unique history in a newspaper article. In the *Bisbee Daily Review* interview, he stated that the old adobe was built by Bill Bueford and George Edwards in the spring of 1881. The two opened a saloon until trouble tore them apart as business partners. Smith said, "This was due to dishonesty and appropriating to their own use as much of the receipts of the saloon as they could get a hold of." Smith added that a fight lasted several days, with threats that resulted in a physical altercation between the two.

In June 1881, the two met at the post office, where Bueford drew his six-shooter and opened fire on Edwards. After the shooter emptied his gun, one of the bullets hit the infamous Black Jack and another unnamed gambler. Fortunately, these were only flesh wounds. Black Jack was shot in the hip, and the other person was shot in the foot. At that point, Edwards drew his gun and fired several shots at Bueford, hitting him in the arm. Edwards was not hit. Bueford was put on trial but was found not guilty, while Edwards was sentenced to five years in prison.

Before heading out to the Yuma Prison to serve his time, Edwards threatened Pete Devore, who had been a member of the jury. After Edwards served his time, he traveled to Russellville in the Dragoon Mountains, where Devore was living. Edwards was determined to keep the promise to kill the man.

On the night Edwards arrived in town, he headed over to Devore's boardinghouse to do just that. Devore saw him first and shot and killed him. Devore was later acquitted on the grounds that Edwards had previously threatened to kill him.

After that debacle, the original saloon was closed. That same year, a flood washed out part of the front and near rear of the building. Repairs were made, and a butcher shop replaced the saloon owned by James Burnett. The adobe was used for several other businesses until 1902, when it became the St. Elmo Saloon.

John Smith, the Bisbee pioneer, stated in his interview that this was the oldest building in the city at the time of the article and had withstood several floods and three or four fires. Each time there was little damage to the building, and it was always immediately repaired.

During the month of January 1903, a newspaper article reported on a serious altercation between two Black men at St. Elmo. E.B. Scott had a serious squabble with Richard Parker, who ran a lunch stand called Yellow Dick inside the bar. Just before nine o'clock in the evening, the two got into a gunfight that also involved razors. They were fighting over Scott's wife. Parker had apparently paid her too much attention.

The two men met behind the saloon, where Parker fired three shots at Scott. He shot him in the left arm and broke it and struck him in the stomach, causing a serious flesh wound. Scott used a razor in the fight and managed to cut his opponent behind his left ear.

Constables Doyle and Casad happened to be walking by and apprehended Parker and placed him under arrest. He was held in a doctor's office, where an officer was placed. Parker was kept there until Scott was released from the hospital. This is when Parker's hearing was to take place. The officers did find the gun near a barn in the alley at the back of St. Elmo but never found the razor.

Scott had a broken arm and a near-fatal wound to his abdomen. The bullet didn't go through his torso, but it went just deep enough to follow the skin partly around one side of his body, then discharged. Scott refused to say who started the terrible fight, but when he was taken away from the area, he was in a wild rage of anger and in a great deal of pain.

After some investigation, it was found that when Scott's wife was packing to leave town the day before the incident, he made a remark about her spending too much time and being seemingly close with Parker. At one time, Scott ran another lunch counter at St. Elmo, and before that he was in the freight business in Phoenix. Police found that Scott had been having the same kind of trouble with his wife for some time due to the way she acted with other men in Bisbee.

Scott had a court hearing soon after the fight and was initially charged with assault to commit murder, but the evidence against him was not enough to warrant it. He was instead charged with assault and battery.

During the crowded court proceedings, the public was disappointed to not hear much about the domestic situation concerning the two men and a woman. John Seymour testified that he was in St. Elmo when he saw Parker fall into the saloon through a door after three gunshots were fired. He said he immediately left after that. His brother William Seymour testified that he had seen Scott buy a flask of whiskey and then walk straight through the saloon and out back. He also said he heard Parker tell him he didn't want any trouble, then Scott responded that Parker had broken up his family.

Eventually, Parker was put on the stand and said he had gone to the door just to talk to Scott. Then Scott attacked him. He testified that, at first, he couldn't tell if he was cut with a knife or a razor and didn't recall seeing anything in his assailant's hands. He only felt himself being cut on the neck.

J.W. Farris testified in court that he had walked by the two men, who were standing on a porch at the rear of the firehouse, and heard them talking. He didn't expect there to be trouble, so he kept walking, then he heard three shots and saw Scott fall from the porch.

Dr. Edmundson told the court that he had tended to Parker, who was cut on the left side of the neck, just below his ear. The wound was just over a half an inch deep and was three-quarters of an inch long. He said that at first he thought it was caused by a bullet but later concluded that it was done with a sharp object.

Scott himself testified that after some words were exchanged, Parker shot at him, and he clinched up. Scott then said that he reached around Parker's neck with a broken whiskey bottle he had in his hand, explaining how the man was cut. Scott also claimed that he had been shot in the stomach before he attempted to make a pass at Parker. Parker was not convicted, but over the next several months, Scott was reported to be in more trouble with the law, including beating a woman who was not his wife.

In August 1903, a strange situation unfolded at St. Elmo. A miner had rushed into the bar around eight in the morning and pulled his gun on a group of men playing cards. The gunman pointed his Colt .45 at the same men he claimed had cheated him out of money several hours before in a game of draw poker. Most of the players at the table were more of a support group for the grafters, and the heated miner was only after the money he was owed.

According to the article in the *Bisbee Daily Review*, "Stranger Makes Bold Stand for His Own in St. Elmo's Saloon by Pulling a Gun on Grafters," the game had been going on for several hours when poker players found themselves staring down the barrel of a six-shooter.

The miner demanded the entire pot of chips, worth $130, but the dealer could only find $60. The gunman was so enraged that the card players thought they were going to be shot and killed right then and there.

Bisbee Police officer Thomas had been called and rushed into St. Elmo and immediately talked the miner into lowering his gun. The miner, in a harsh and stern voice, told the officer that they were cheaters and he was only there to get what was his. Officer Thomas told the miner, who was now much calmer, that he'd get to the bottom of the situation, and then he let him leave.

A reporter called St. Elmo later that day to inquire about the situation and was told that they didn't know of anything like that happening there. An employee did say that when he showed up for work that morning, things did seem out of sort. He said that cards were thrown all over the floor and the barkeeper was shaky and acting very nervous. The reporter stated that with such suspicious evidence, he couldn't believe that there wasn't anything worth talking about and figured the owners didn't want their regulars to be put off and lose customers.

When St. Elmo relocated to Brewery Avenue, it moved into a two-story building and continued to do very well with the townspeople. It was also a perfect place to put prized possessions on display. D.T. Greene in 1908 brought steer horns from Cananea, Mexico, that measured three and a half feet from tip to tip. The owners of the establishment hung them over the center of the bar.

In 1910, it was reported that a pelican was killed in the San Pedro Valley area and was said to be the only one ever shot down in the southwestern desert at that time. Jake Baker was a local rancher and was the man who shot it out of the sky near the river. There were two, but the other one was severely mangled and not suitable for mounting. A Bisbee taxidermist mounted the bird, and Baker sold it to O.S. French, who had it on exhibition at the St. Elmo Bar. Baker had stated to a local paper that the Pelicans were caught in a high wind and were pushed over the San Pedro River.

Years went by, and more peculiar and traumatic incidents continued to unfold at St. Elmo. By 1908, the establishment had made the upstairs into a lodging area. A St. Elmo bartender staying in one of the rooms named N.O. Walker committed suicide because he was afraid that he was becoming insane. The forty-year-old barkeeper took poison at around eight in the morning. Other roomers said they heard loud groans coming from his room, as if the man was in a great degree of pain. When the witnesses went into his room, they found Walker in a horrible state. Dr. Hawley was called and, when he arrived, could see there was no saving the man's life. The doctor still attempted to revive him. Walker lost consciousness, and the doctor was not successful.

Several of Walker's friends said he had told them on different occasions while he bartended that he was going to kill himself. He thought it was best if he took morphine and ended it all. This is the drug Dr. Hawley and Coroner Hogan suspected was the cause of death.

Another suicide took place in 1919 in the same lodging area, but in a much more violent way. An article in the *Bisbee Daily Review* reported that James C. Dale, a carpenter, had dinner and, after the meal, went to bed in one of the rooms upstairs. When he didn't wake up when called the next morning, the door was forced open, and a horrendous sight was seen. Dale was found lying in a pool of blood with a gunshot wound to his head. He still had the .45-caliber revolver in his hand that did the deed. An examination of the cause of death determined he had been dead for at least three or four hours before being found.

Witnesses stated that they did hear a muffled gunshot at about 4:00 a.m. but ignored it. Dale was discovered around 7:00 a.m. Coroner J.L. Winters and Constable Sheppard investigated his room and decided he had come to his death from gunshot wounds inflicted by his own hand. No motive for the suicide was ever known. He was forty-two.

During 1909, one of the more bizarre sides of the bar's history involved two men who made an outlandish ten-dollar bet. The *Bisbee Daily Review* reported that Felix Finley and Matt Dillon, well known in Bisbee, came up with a dangerous stunt. In a conversation between the men, Finley bragged that during his adventurous and wild days as a youngster, he was a balloonist and parachute expert. He said he had often risked his life to do parachute drops. He was so daring that he would leap from tall buildings with just an umbrella and would float gently to the ground. Dillon didn't believe a word of it, and the two began a heated argument, resulting in the bet. Finley offered ten dollars that he could jump off the St. Elmo building unharmed. Dillon looked at the building, which was about fifty feet tall, and instantly agreed to the bet.

The settling of the bet was to be held on a Sunday, but the Bisbee Police caught wind of it and showed up before it could be accomplished. The police stopped Finley from going through with what they thought would be certain death for the daredevil.

Regardless of what the police thought, Finley was determined to do the leap of death as soon as he could get the authorities off his back and was more than willing to go through with it. Dillon was positive that the jump would be fatal, and although he thought of Finley as one of his dearest friends, he needed the ten dollars. His only regret about the bet was that he was positive that within ten seconds from the time his friend left the roof and on his downward flight, he would become an angel and would not be around to admit that for once his judgment was wrong.

About two weeks later, another article was published in the same newspaper, stating that Fenley had decided to put his fate in his own hands and took on the wager. He decided to jump off not the St. Elmo building but instead the Shattuck building. With umbrella in hand, he looked at his friend below and gave him a smile, then leaped off the edge of the roof with both hands secured tightly to the stick.

Astonishingly, instead of Finley floating down to the sidewalk, he found himself soaring into the air. He went higher every second. Dillon's mouth dropped, but he thought quick and grabbed a rope and lassoed his friend around his foot. Dillon was able to pull Finley down to the roof. But the story doesn't stop there. Finley couldn't explain the phenomenon except that probably the law of gravitation had disappeared. He was game to try again. He insisted Dillon hang on to the rope, which was now tied around his leg. He stepped to the edge of the roof and jumped again, but with the same result! The article stated that as soon as he made the leap, he started to float toward the blue sky once again.

It was reported that when he was pulled down by the now-exhausted Dillon and landed on the roof, Finley started for the sidewalk to determine what was happening to him. When he reached the pavement, he immediately saw the problem. Directly below where he had tried to make

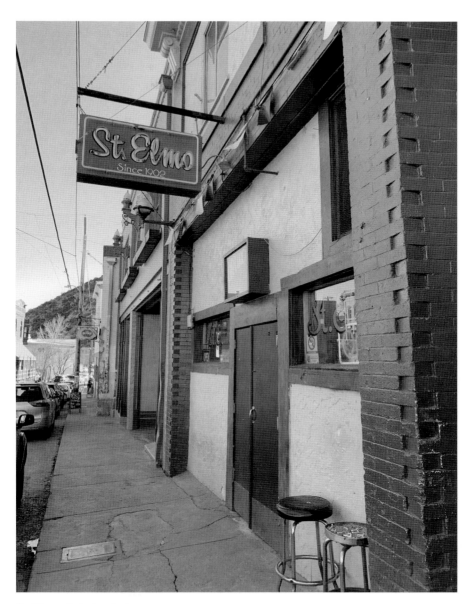

St. Elmo. *Author's collection.*

the leap, three local men, Roy Morfoot, Carl Graf and a man named Edmunds, were in deep conversation about baseball and how they used to play when they were children.

Finley groaned and turned to Dillon and said: "No chance for me to make good. I can't come down with the umbrella while all that hot air is going up." The newspaper added that Finley would try again later, but not until he was positive those men would be safely tucked away on their couches at night.

Legend says part of an old bordello called the Blair House is the third story of the present building. Rumor has it that several men carried the small structure from farther up the Gulch and placed it on the roof of St. Elmo. They did that to have a more convenient place for their contribution to the tenderloin business.

St. Elmo is still in business and has recently been recognized as a "Historic Dive Bar" by the National Trust for Historic Preservation. According to *Arizona Highways*, St. Elmo was one of seven dive bars honored by the organization as part of a recent National Dive Bar Day. The online blog stated, "The National Trust says such businesses 'are an integral part of America's historic character,' in that they emulate the love and energy we put into our communities."

6

BISBEE AND LOWELL'S RED-LIGHT DISTRICT

*I*n Upper Brewery Gulch, there was another sort of business expanding and gaining momentum. This area was called the Red-Light District. Soon after Bisbee was named, city officials tried to control prostitution without prohibiting it.

In 1892, the Board of Supervisors of Cochise County adopted a law that confined all brothels to a designated area of South Main Street and west of OK Street. Then, in 1897, to place it at a distance from the homes of families and respectable wives, mothers and children, the Red-Light District was designated to Upper Brewery Gulch and later extended to a part of Zacatecas Canyon.

One of the major factors in Bisbee's incorporation as a city in 1902 was the regulation of vice and brothels. The first act of the new municipality was to ban women from saloons. Despite that, there were over thirty designated spots for hiring women of ill repute in the Red-Light District. There were also opium dens, hop-joints, casinos, cribs and "supposed" boardinghouses. Mexican national and Mexican American families lived in the same borough.

The prostitutes endured a crude lifestyle, and it brought brutal consequences, which often put them in dire straits. Among the acts of violence and criminality in this part of town were murders, fights and brawls that sometimes lasted for days, horrific and graphic treatment of young (and sometimes old) women, property damage, theft and even fires.

On the other hand, Bisbee women working in the tenderloin business were given mandatory health tests. The Cochise County Hygiene Board

Prostitute holding a shot of whiskey called Raleigh Rye from New Orleans, circa 1912. *Photo attributed to E.J. Bellocq Wikimedia Commons.*

boasted that the Bisbee girls would pass with A-plus grades. Among the regular visitors to the Red-Light District were U.S. Army soldiers from Camp Naco and the Douglas post nearby. This was great for business, but by 1910, prostitution was completely restricted in Bisbee. With that, prostitutes, their pimps and the owners of whorehouses were said to have packed up and left in groups on the train to El Paso. By April 1, 1910, the era of "Wild Brewery Gulch" was over.

Although the existence of the Red-Light District had ended in the Upper Brewery Gulch and Zacatecas areas, Lowell had its own. That started around 1904 and lasted until the winter of 1917. The U.S. secretary of war investigated how the women working in Lowell were affecting the soldiers stationed nearby. The secretary directed the city of Bisbee to close Lowell's Red-Light District. The city council complied and voted to close the tenderloin district on December 10, 1917.

THE TENDERLOIN WAS A LUCRATIVE BISBEE BUSINESS

Prostitution has always been a lucrative business, and that was no different in Bisbee. The mining camp was full of prospective customers, married or not. Those involved could be heavily fined for several different types of crimes associated with the profession. The many houses of ill repute and other businesses that housed the women of the tenderloin such as gambling halls and various saloons were all making tons of cash and paid lots of taxes. Author Robert Dykstra wrote in his book *The Cattle Towns* that the aim of most civic authorities was local regulation rather than prohibition. He added, "The accomplishment of those goals created constant demands on law enforcement and town councils, which in turn enhanced the public roles and authority of civic institutions."

Author Anne Butler wrote in her book *Daughters of Joy, Sisters of Misery* that Bisbee attempted to control the business of the tenderloin without making it illegal. Bisbee was part of Cochise County, with Tombstone the county seat, at this time. Butler used Tombstone as an example of how empowering and self-serving relationships between officialdom and peddlers of vice worked. The police and sheriff's offices were full of untrained and corruptible individuals, which in turn gave great opportunity for self-profit and induced power.

An example of how lucrative prostitution can be involves one of the most notorious soiled doves of the mining town. Bisbee's Little Irish Mag was so successful that she became a madame. According to the book *Brewery Gulch: Frontier Days of Old Arizona, Last Outpost of the Great Southwest* by Joe Chisholm, she lived in a green-roofed house on Main Street. She had a green parrot who picked up the rugged language from the miners and mule skinners who frequented her business. She walked up and down the street freely, except when a respectable woman, such as a mining executive's wife, was about to pass by. An unspoken rule among prostitutes was to make themselves disappear and either run into a saloon or hide behind a wall, whatever it took so that a presentable woman wouldn't have to lay their eyes on them. Although the prostitutes weren't seen, they did look at passing women to see what the latest fashions were for an eloquent lady.

Because one of the richest and most famous claims in Bisbee was named for her (the Irish Mag Mine of the Calumet & Arizona Mining Company) and developed into one if not the most successful mines in the area, she has gone down in infamy. Chisholm suggested that Mag might have helped with the financing of the claim. If this is true, not only did she have a place in the hearts of a man who thought enough of her to name such a rich claim in her honor, but it is also speculated that she had the funds to invest and harvest the mining industry's vast success.

I do have to add that county officials admitted to collecting money for the vice licenses, but they also paid out hundreds of dollars in justice and constable fees to preserve the peace and quiet of the Red-Light District.

Another problem arose often, since Bisbee is on the international border with Mexico and immigration situations were present. Some of the madams would be caught bringing young girls over from Mexico for "immoral purposes." Then women were put in front of a grand jury and held in jail until released or convicted.

THE SCARLET GIRLS OF THE GULCH

The scarlet girls of Brewery Gulch have been documented as successful businesswomen and portrayed as compassionate and endearing figures. Many of these women used the money they earned to help people in need in their town. Some left that lifestyle and married, had children and celebrated another world of living altogether. Even though it was not illegal to work as a prostitute during the years before the incorporated city laws changed that, it still was frowned on.

The women of the tenderloin community also had to endure battles among themselves. Fights among the women, violent affairs that included knives, guns and anything in arm's reach, were all part of the culture. The

Remnants of sets of stairs from Mable's Crib. A place of ill repute from over one hundred years ago located in what used to be Bisbee's Red-Light District. Prostitution cribs are described as structures whose facades are arranged into a series of narrow bays, each of which has an individual door entry. This would have been just one place where the Scarlet Girls of the Gulch worked. *Author's collection.*

prostitutes in Bisbee found ways to identify with other trades in order to live in disguise and hide what they were really undertaking as working women in the underworld. They would identify as seamstresses, easily blending in with legitimate career women. It isn't uncommon to see in censuses at the turn of the twentieth century women of a young age being single and living in lodging houses with several others. They would also be listed as living with one older female and have dressmaking as their occupation.

Nevertheless, the women of the Gulch lived and worked in various forms of service. Some of the girls didn't work in the deep trade of prostitution but only shared a drink or a dance and worked in a gambling, drinking or music hall as servers. These were all known to be part of the harlotry era that started on Main Street and then moved to Brewery Gulch, then located finally in the burrows of Upper Brewery Avenue.

ANITA ROMERO

There is one woman who stands out in the tenderloin of the Gulch: Anita Romero. Chisholm stated that Romero ran one of the most successful and wildest disreputable establishments in Upper Brewery Gulch. She is described as a Mexican national. With her exotic features and olive-colored skin, along with her long dark hair, she was one of the most sought-after and fought-over women of ill repute in the Gulch.

Romero may have come to the United States around 1899 at around twenty-five years of age. It was thought that she had worked in Bisbee since her teens and continued until she was thirty. She was in the newspaper often and was involved in several situations that required her to be called as a witness to testify at inquests. She spoke very little, broken English, which may have caused interpretation problems for her.

In December 1900, a Mexican man was a victim of an assault at Romero's establishment. He had a bullet in his neck and a large slash from a knife in his back. The next year, in January, another man, Pedro Ariola, was arrested and taken to Tombstone, where he was going to be indicted on a charge of murder. He was accused of killing another man at Romero's place.

There was more trouble at Romero's establishment just a couple of weeks later. The *Cochise Review* reported on January 26, 1901, that there was another killing there. A man named Abundio Salas was shot and killed by Deputy Constable Francisco Jurado, who had just been deputized by Constable Doyle on January 2.

Several witnesses testified during an inquest at the Justice Court for the murder. They said that Officer Doyle and Deputy Constable Johnson were called to Romero's place of business at 9:00 p.m. on the twenty-first by Deputy Constable Jurado. When they arrived, some of Romero's women reported that four Mexicans had threatened to go to the establishment and were going to rough it up. At that point, two men from the group were in the barroom and for some time used vile and malicious language to the bartender and to the people surrounding them. Doyle stated that he searched the men and found no weapons. He also said he instructed Jurado to take charge and arrest anyone who became disruptive, as he and Johnson were being called elsewhere. Doyle stated that he felt Jurado had everything under control.

According to the testimony, the senior officers made their way to downtown, when they heard four rapid successions of gunshots near Shattuck's lumberyard. The last shot, according to Doyle's capability of deciphering the difference, sounded like two guns were involved. The two officers ran back toward the sounds of the gunfire and found a dead body in the road about one hundred yards from the lumberyard. Deputy Constable Jurado was standing over the body.

Jurado said, "He tried to kill me, and I shot him." Doyle stated that there was a .38-caliber pistol lying about ten feet from the dead man with three empty chambers just recently discharged. The officer placed Jurado under arrest and took his gun that had recently emptied one chamber. He addressed the jury and asked them to thoroughly investigate the matter and circumstances leading to the killings. He explained the necessity of having an officer regularly stationed in the immediate vicinity of the disreputable places in Upper Brewery Gulch.

Jurado testified that his orders as a new officer were to remain in the close vicinity of the disreputable houses and to especially take every precaution against the carrying of deadly weapons in the vicinity. Justice Williams addressed Jurado and said that it appeared to him that he was acting in self-defense and released him from custody. Salas was shot in the right part of his chest, leaving him with a large, deep wound. He was reported to have been in Bisbee only a few days after coming from Jerome.

Romero was also arrested on occasion for being drunk and fighting and became the spotlight for the core of trouble in Upper Brewery Gulch. Another incident involved her employees. Officer Johnson had been called to her establishment to arrest a drunken Mexican national. When he entered, all the women working on that day jumped him. They beat him up, but he was able to get away and left to get his gun. He brought Officer Foster back with him and arrested the women and put them in jail. They were eventually released but heavily fined for their actions.

A blurb was written in the *Cochise News* stating that steps should be taken by Bisbee police to close Romero's establishment. The week before the article, the place was a scene of a shooting and stabbings. It had become a sort of headquarters for men who were constantly drunk and violent. The large number of individuals hanging around the establishment may have been due to the laborers in the area who were part of the construction of the South Western Railroad. The writer of the blurb stated that there were several unwritten laws in force in Bisbee and believed the removal of this nest of hard characters should be place on the statutes.

According to an article written by Bob Newman retrieved from the Bisbee Mining & Historical Museum, Romero was upset that many young men had their romantic relationships broken up due to their girlfriend or wife finding out they had visited her place. Newman wrote that on her leaving Bisbee, she gave her many patrons an enchilada banquet, withdrew all her money and with her children (whose fathers she didn't know the identities of) went back to Mexico to live in Cananea.

DEBAUCHERY

Let's dive a little more into the "trouble" side of the scarlet girls in the Gulch. In local newspapers, there was no lack of reports on the doings of the tenderloin in Bisbee. In 1911, there was a doozy of a brawl there. On a Friday night, there was an inter-house conflict, where it was reported that blood flowed freely from those who participated and that they had black eyes to match by the time Officers McRae and Trotter came on the scene.

Two scarlet girls, Marie Hoppe and Doris Tyson, were arrested for fighting each other and fined $25. This was the judge's way of forcing peace among the women and to punish them for their annoyance. Hoppe was also handed a warrant for a complaint made by a woman named Hester Barker. Barker claimed Hoppe was threatening her life. Hoppe was placed under a cash bond of $250. In turn, Hoppe made a claim against Tempest Wyland and was arrested. Wyland pleaded not guilty and was set free.

Another disturbance in Upper Brewery Gulch is described as a free-for-all. Evelyn Waddell was attacked, beaten and choked by a man named J.W. Skeels. The man was sentenced to serve thirty-five days in the city jail, not for assaulting Waddell, but he was serving the time for disturbing the peace. Waddell was fined seventy-five dollars for the charge of vagrancy.

In 1908, May Jerome was working in the Red-Light District, and a man named Sam Bowers hit her. It was reported that Bowers was drinking heavily and seemed to be in the mood for a fight. When Jerome tried to calm him down and put her hands on him in an oh-so-sweet way, he returned her affection with a straight punch in the face. Bowers was arrested.

In October of the same year, a Black woman working in the tenderloin of Bisbee, Nellie Burns, took out her knife and tried to stab another African American woman, Belle Walker. The victim was only slightly injured, but Officers James and Ed Stevens arrested Burns for the assault.

Walker was in the newspaper the following year, in 1909. This time, it was reported that the woman from the Red-Light District and at the end of Brewery Avenue (Upper Brewery Gulch) was charged for using obscene language in public. A Black man named Frank Lewis owned and ran a shoeshine stand at the corner where the Miner Store was located. Lewis claimed in front of the justice of the high court that Walker cursed him out while he was busy shining the shoes of a customer. He even brought in the customer to prove his accusation.

Lewis also alleged that Walker said she was in the habit of giving him a thrashing with her tongue every time she happened to see him. A ten-dollar bench warrant was made, and Walker was arrested by Officer McRae.

Unfortunately, there was a period of years during which a long string of girls and women were so distraught in the life of prostitution that they tried to commit suicide. During the early part of December 1913, a few women were left working as prostitutes. This is when it was reported that Jean Williams was found on the floor of her room, unconscious.

A small group of her friends were knocking at her door on a Sunday at 1:00 p.m. As they called her name, they detected the strong odor of natural gas. When they broke down the door, they found not only Williams but also a disconnected gas hose and realized the room was full of the gas. Williams was given emergency medical care, and after two hours, regained consciousness. The young woman admitted she had tried to kill herself but never gave a reason why.

Then there were women in the district who were so admired by customers that they claimed love and marriage for themselves. During the summer of 1912, a Bisbee man named Albert Telley was determined to marry a French national woman named Lily Silver. Telley claimed to have met her in New York before coming to Bisbee.

The nineteen-year-old French woman, seven months before, had been taken out of a house of prostitution in the Gulch. She traveled to New York from France along with two other French girls and two Frenchmen. The *Bisbee Daily Review* reported that at the time she arrived in the United States, she claimed she was a virgin and was brought to this country with the understanding that she would get paid well as a waitress. Silver claimed she had been a waitress for two years in her home country.

She was soon arrested and deported to France for violation of the federal statute forbidding women traveling to this country for immoral purposes. Eventually, she came back to the United States and made it to Buffalo, New York. She came through Canada and then traveled to San Francisco, then finally to Bisbee.

City Marshal Ed Stevens was told she was in town and, with an immigration inspector named Charles Connell from Douglas, placed her in custody. The

Washington, D.C. office instructed her to be taken to Tucson, where she was to be put on trial.

Telley told Officer Frank Johnson the day after her arrest that he was going to marry the girl. His plan was to go to Tucson to marry "Lily." The young man wanted to know if as a result of that he could keep her from being deported. Officer Johnson didn't have the answer to that question but said that the opinion of the officials might be lenient in such a case. Telley was determined to travel to Tucson and marry her.

The real name of the French woman was not known, but the reporter described Silver as a striking type of a French beauty who spoke with broken English. When she was arrested, she had over a dozen letters from a wealthy man in Los Angeles, asking her to be his bride. According to government authorities, in this case they were on a hunt for Silver to secure the conviction of the two Frenchmen she traveled with. These men were known to have a profitable business of bringing young girls to the United States for the purpose of prostitution.

MAY GILLIS'S HOUSE OF ILL REPUTE

A woman named May Brown (alias May Gillis) was arrested for running a brothel at the top of Broadway Avenue, now called the Broadway Stairs. An article in the *Bisbee Daily Review* of April 23, 1912, "Raid House That Is near a School—Immoral Place Can't Be Run within 400 Yards of Public School," reported that a residence on Broadway had been raided by City Marshal Bassett Watkins and Night Officer Walter Brooks on April 21. The residence had been under investigation for some time, and when it was raided in the early part of the day, two individuals were arrested for keeping and residing in houses for "immoral" purposes located within four hundred yards of a school. Unfortunately for them, the school was less than fifty yards from the Central School.

May Gillis pleaded guilty and was sentenced to pay a fine of fifty dollars. She ended up at the County Branch Jail for fifty days because she couldn't pay the fine. The other person arrested was Victor Sitner. He pleaded not guilty and demanded a trial, which was set for April 26. He was released on bond for twenty-five dollars.

Gillis had a ruffian reputation and a depressing past. In 1905, she was staying at the Elite Lodging House on Main Street and mistakenly drank carbolic acid. The newspaper reported that she claimed she had a very bad headache in the middle of the night and made the mistake of drinking the entire bottle of the acid, mistaking it for medicine she had in her room.

Some say that this was no accident and that she instead tried to kill herself. Despite the pain in her mouth and throat from the fiery acid, she was able to produce banshee-like screams of anguish that saved her life. Somebody was able to get her help in time. She ended up in jail a few times after that, including for trying to shoot Sitner. Sadly, she was committed to the asylum by the Lunacy Commission, composed of D.H.H. Hughart and C.R. Baker, in 1916.

Mrs. Henry Savage

The story of Kate Gordon Savage was one of the most terrible and tragic tales of a woman who left the underworld for a more "normalized" life. She shot and killed her husband in front of their house and afterward showed absolutely no remorse and instead rejoiced when his death was confirmed.

Kate Savage was reported to formerly be a mistress of a house of ill repute in Brewery Gulch. She was better known as Mildred Ray. This may have been her real name. Prostitutes often changed their names. According to the *Bisbee Daily Review*, she was married to Henry and was living in the Wood Canyon neighborhood of Tombstone Canyon. Henry was a forty-two-year-old employee of the St. Elmo Bar on Brewery Gulch and a member of the Order of Eagles and was from Portsmouth, Ohio. He had arrived in Bisbee two years before his death.

The married couple and the woman's sons from another marriage lived at the home. Her son Albert Stone from Tucson arrived a few days before the shooting to take over a new laundry business the couple owned. The pair had been relentlessly feuding over the management and the funds needed for their enterprise. Henry was not happy with the decision by Stone to take over and warned the son not to come. For several days before the unpleasant incident, Henry drank heavily and allegedly abused his wife. He threatened to kill her several times until she left the house to stay with neighbors. She even stayed one night on a hillside with her eight-month-old baby, because she was terrified of Henry.

The evening of the murder, Henry Savage was walking up a trail leading to their house with a six-shooter in his right-hand hip pocket and with a bottle of whiskey. As he made his way closer to the house, Kate appeared at a window and yelled at him to stop. She said she saw him reach for his gun. Unfortunately for him, she was holding a shotgun and was an excellent markswoman.

She fired the gun and hit him directly in the forehead, killing him almost instantly. She told the newspaper that her younger son Amos ran to the door of the house with a rifle, but she said to him: "Don't shoot, Amos! I have already killed him."

The double-barreled shotgun and the full charge of one barrel entered the man's head just above the forehead, traveled through the brain and came out at the back of the head, tearing away the skull. Immediately after, Kate asked one of her sons to hitch up their wagon and was driven to the office of Justice of the Peace C.A. McDonald, where she surrendered herself to a deputy sheriff.

Henry's body was kept at the Hennessy Parlor, where many friends and acquaintances went to visit the remains. Most of those individuals seemed to be there only out of morbid curiosity. They were reported to not just stand by his side and say their goodbyes but also pulled back the sheet covering his face to look at the horrific wounds and trauma to his head. The funeral for the man was held under the auspices of the Order of Eagles.

The woman was arrested, and the deputy who was putting her in her cell said he regretted having to do so. Kate Savage said, "Never mind about that, when there is occasion for it, I can be just as nervy as any of them."

During Kate's preliminary examination, through testimony it was shown that Amos Stone had been in a barn near the house with a rifle. What appeared to be a rifle bullet hole was discovered in Henry's hat. The entrance point indicated that the bullet had come from the direction opposite to where Kate was positioned. The only explanation was that it came from the rifle Amos Stone was holding and that, by incredible chance, the two guns went off at the same time, explaining no witnesses said they heard two gunshots.

Most of the witnesses who testified regurgitated the same instances of Henry's behavior of heavy drinking and violent anger that resulted at one point in him breaking several pieces of furniture in his home during a rage of madness. The witnesses agreed that the Savages had been having domestic problems for some time. Neighbors said that on different occasions, Kate repeated to them that she was afraid the situation would eventually end badly.

Amos Stone gave an interesting statement during the hearing. He said: "What I did in this matter I had to do and would do it over again if I had to. A man who will not protect his mother is a mighty poor man."

C.L. Jones, owner of the St. Elmo, testified that Henry worked as a bartender for him, and he knew the man to be quiet and peaceable. Jones said that Henry told him he had invested $1,500 in his laundry business and wanted to get out of it. On cross-examination, Jones said he had only seen him slap a man's face once and knew he carried a gun at times. He didn't know anything about Henry's relationship with his wife.

A neighbor named Lula Brown testified that she heard another neighbor, Mrs. O'Connor, yell, 'Guessed they've killed old man Savage and it's a good thing as he has threatened all our lives." William Brown testified that after he heard the shot, he saw how the body was positioned. He said, "It lay on its face with arms outstretched, with a package of some kind clasped in its hand." Winifred Harris swore that on the same afternoon of the murder she saw Amos bring a rifle out of a car and go with it into the barn. After the shot was fired, she saw Amos run out of the barn with the rifle and at the same time saw Kate run out of her house.

After the court proceedings, Justice McDonald committed the mother and son to jail without bond. They were held for a trial before the grand jury for murder. Amos Stone was now arrested for being an accessory to the murder. The trial was moved to Santa Cruz County at Nogales, where Judge Doan presided. Kate's attorney won the request for the change of venue in December 1905 for a fair trial, as the case had been sensationalized and was covered heavily by the press in Cochise County. It was moved to Nogales.

On October 17, 1906, Savage was acquitted of the charge of murder. The jury was out for only one hour before a verdict was reached. Amos Stone's case was dismissed thereafter.

7

BISBEE'S PIONEER CEMETERY AND ZACATECAS

During the early development of Bisbee, people were rushing in to be part of the rapid growth and success resulting from the newly founded wealth overflowing from the mining industry. At the time, the population was mostly made up of men. These men had traveled not only from all corners of the United States but also from around the world. They came alone, leaving family and friends behind. Some of those men were buried in the town's first cemetery, with no flowers or any kind of gifts left on their graves. This is one of the reasons the pioneer cemetery became Bisbee's City Park. The cemetery lies between Opera Drive and Brewery Avenue and was established in the late 1880s. The logistics surrounding the eventual transition from cemetery to park happened decades later and includes the critical neglect of the graves, which also involved speculation regarding the contamination of water wells upslope from the property.

A very enlightening article in the *Bisbee Daily Review* from 1913 included a collage of photographs showing the outrageous sight of laundry being dried on the fencing of graves in the cemetery. Other plots were in shambles, falling apart and full of overgrown weeds. This demonstrated the lack of care and respect for those interred there. Neighborhood children played in the hazardous area, causing more worry and woe from people who lived in the Gulch.

By 1910, the city council had begun to hear complaints about the cemetery and demands that they find a solution to the danger zone. That same year, a petition was presented by I.W. Wallace on behalf of the board

The actual pioneer cemetery before the site was made into Bisbee's City Park. *Author's collection.*

of education to the city council to use the site of the old cemetery for a building to segregate children of African descent. Plans were eventually brought to the council, but it was the voice of the board and Bisbee residents to choose the property for a playground instead. Children were already using the old cemetery as a play area. If they weren't playing there, they would be running in the very narrow streets, barely avoiding cars, horses and wagons. It was a very chaotic and unsafe situation that was in dire need of a resolution.

A Playground Committee was formed by the Commercial Club to plan for a park for the neighborhood children. An article in the *Bisbee Daily Review* with the headline "Dilapidated Graveyard or Playground, Which?" described members of the committee during a council meeting explaining the law regarding city and town cemeteries enacted by the legislative assembly of the territory of Arizona. The law read that whenever any ground used as a cemetery within city limits has been abandoned and ceases to be used for such purposes, is unfit or unsuited or becomes obnoxious and can be used for other public purposes to better advantage, the city or town's use of the grounds was to be vacated. The remains of the persons buried there are to be removed to some other cemetery or suitable place. The expense of such removal was to be paid by the city or town.

Above: Handwritten log sheet for the graves at the pioneer cemetery. Note John Tappiner listed. He was a victim of the Bisbee Massacre. *Author's collection.*

Left: City Park cornerstone. *Author's collection.*

The law also read that whenever the remains are removed, all monuments and gravestones were also to be removed and replaced at the new cemetery. The graves were to be numbered and a list of the names of the buried kept. The question of abandonment of the old cemetery was made easily. During a special meeting of the City Council in January 1913,

Secretary Gray of the Commercial Club said: "We want to place all of these bodies where they will be decently cared for, where the graves will be kept as they should be. We want no desecration of graves but on the contrary, want them made sacred."

Money was raised to renovate the neglected monstrosity, to move the bodies buried in the pioneer burial ground to a new one in Lowell called Evergreen Cemetery and to buy playground equipment. Some residents were nervous that not all the bodies were removed, but there was a diplomatic and vigilant transfer of the graves to Evergreen Cemetery before the construction and landscaping of the park began. Thirty-four bodies were removed and relocated; twenty-three of those were identified. The last recorded person to be buried there was in 1898, the infant son of H.M. Woods.

The City Park had a formal dedication on May 20, 1916, with Governor Hunt in attendance. Memorial Day, the Fourth of July, important political meetings and an array of other events were celebrated here. The city also used the public park for ceremonies for draftees leaving for war.

Decapitated Human Head Found

On the wicked side of Bisbee's past, an unbelievable piece of history includes a human head, with no regard or respect about to whom it belonged. It had been abandoned in Bisbee's pioneer cemetery. This revolting event was reported in the *Bisbee Daily Review* on April 16, 1913. It was the most ghastly and gruesome story ever told about that location. According to the article, the head was brought from a battle during the Naco Engagement and its theater of war.

At midmorning, Chief of Police Watkins received a phone call from a very emotional person who said Watkins should get up to the cemetery immediately. The caller hung up before Watkins could ask about the situation and why it what so urgent. Despite the lack of information, Watkins made his way from the police station and headed toward the cemetery.

As he stepped closer to the grave site, he could hear several loud voices chatting in excitement. Going through the entrance gate, Watkins saw a curiously large crowd. Many of the individuals were children, and they were all standing in a tight circle, looking at the ground. Watkins's heart pumped hard as he made his way into the mass of people, trying to see what the commotion was about. As soon as he caught sight of what everyone was looking at, his mouth flew open. A human head was lying on the dirt in a revolting state of decomposition. The head was of a man, barely recognizable as a human and devastating to look at.

A police investigation was conducted, and it was found that the head was thought to be a souvenir and brought up from Naco. A pair of men had apparently brought it to a saloon down on Brewery Gulch and wanted it to be displayed. Fortunately, the owner of the saloon thought that was a very bad idea and didn't want it in his bar.

The owner had the head taken to the cemetery to be buried in a shallow grave. Unfortunately, it was too shallow, and a neighborhood dog found it. The dog dug it out, and that's when the crowd gathered. Watkins had it buried in a much deeper hole and went as far as making sure the grave site was covered with a large pile of rocks so that it wouldn't be disturbed again. Authorities said they thought the head had been in the cemetery for approximately two weeks.

GEORGE WARREN BURIED TWICE

Another notable person buried there was George Warren. An article from 1905 in the *Bisbee Daily Review* stated that Warren had died in his lonely cabin in 1888 and his body buried in the cemetery in the vicinity of the Bisbee Opera House. In the same paper in March 1914, an article with the headline "Monument to Mark Newly Found Grave of George Warren" stated that in an inconspicuous part of the old cemetery, members of the Bisbee Elks Club found his grave site. They found a worm-eaten and weather-beaten wood headboard with very faint carved letters, "G.W." The Bisbee 82 Elks Club organization investigated and learned that this grave did indeed belong to the infamous George Warren.

According to a 1905 article, "Discoverer George Warren First Locator in District," he was buried in the old cemetery near his home, which was located on Opera Drive, just above the grave site. It was said that good ol' George was buried by a few men who didn't care for the man. (Until his end, George had a nasty reputation.) The burial was not what one would expect, as he was one of the primary founders of Bisbee. Warren was almost tagged as an "unknown" in the cemetery.

A meeting was held by a committee of Bisbee citizens in the general offices of the Copper Queen Company shortly after the discovery of the

George Warren photo taken by the famous Wild West photographer C.S. Fly in a studio in Bisbee. *Author's collection.*

grave. The plan was to raise money for a more "suitable" monument in Evergreen Cemetery. They accomplished that plan, and Warren's grave site has one of the largest tombstones in the graveyard, in glorious fashion. It depicts the larger-than-life prospector whom history writes as a man who blazed the trails in the area and was seen often with his trusty rifle held across his shoulder.

The 1917 George Warren monument in Evergreen Cemetery, built with money collected from the local Elks Club. *Author's collection.*

Here is a little more of Warren's backstory. He had a long life of trauma and drama. The abrasive prospector was born in Massachusetts in about 1835. After his mother died, he joined his father, who was a teamster in New Mexico. A group of renegade Apaches killed his father and held Geoge captive. He lived with the Apaches and witnessed many traumatic things that took place in his presence, including the Apaches burning down homes and stealing cattle. George even saw their enemies being tortured until dead.

He was a young boy at the time and was held for eighteen months by his subjugators. He was traded for fifteen pounds of sugar to two traveling prospectors who recognized him as white. He learned a great deal of prospecting from his two rescuers and later, through odd jobs, gained mining experience.

The first claim in Bisbee was the Rucker Claim and was filed in Pima County in Tucson on August 2, 1877, by Jack Dunn and Lieutenant Rucker. Since the men were actively working for the military, they asked Warren to go to the same canyon to see if he could find more minerals. There was the expectation that all that he found would be shared equally among the men. After the agreement was reached, the prospector was supplied with everything he needed.

Warren was known to be a heavy drinker, so it was no surprise that on his way to the area, which had been mapped out for him, he instead headed to a saloon in the middle of nowhere outside of Tombstone. After a few drinks, he sold everything he was given and went on a binge. He was said to be in that area for a week before he began to recite to two men his quest for silver. He ended up telling them everything and even showed the map he had in his shirt pocket. The two re-grubstaked the prospector, and the three headed out to finish the task. Warren staked fifteen claims of his own and the site where the richest ores were ever found. Only fifty-six days after the Rucker Mine had been discovered, Warren filed a claim, naming it the Mercy Mine. He is considered by some to be the "Father of Bisbee."

Dunn did come back to Bisbee after his stint with the military and thought that Warren was dead, since he had never heard from him. When Dunn came into the same canyon, he found several men locating their own claims. He was disgusted with Warren for being a fraudulent and conniving man. He decided to sell the Rucker Claim for $4,000 and moved back home to Connecticut. He died seven years later.

Close-up of Warren's plaque on his memorial. *Author's collection.*

Years afterward, Warren gambled several claims in a footrace against a horse in Charleston, Arizona. He lost that race and, eventually, the rest of his claims, worth millions of dollars, to deceitful and greedy business partners. In the last years of his life, he worked at different saloons, sweeping floors and cleaning spittoons. Author Opie Rundle Burgess wrote that during the latter days of Warren's life, the Bisbee mortician ordered a particular style of coffin to see if the booming town would be interested in it. The casket was very luxurious, covered in black velour with gilt handles. Inside, it was lined with silk.

The mortician placed the coffin on display outside his building, as he

City Park today and the site of the pioneer cemetery. This is the same point of view as the historical photo. *Author's collection.*

was very excited about the new model. This sparked the attention of an unknown miner on his way to work. He saw it from a distance and crossed the street to get a closer look. As he walked nearer to the casket, he noticed there was a body inside it. It was good ol' George, dead asleep. This was one of the incidents that triggered an investigation into Warren's sanity. Eventually, he was diagnosed as insane and put in an asylum. When he was released, he discovered that his money had been drained and he was now penniless.

He was recorded to have died of pneumonia at the hospital located at the base of Sacramento Hill. In 1917, a grand monument to Warren was placed in Evergreen Cemetery with a plaque reading, "Poor in Purse Rich in Friends." The famous photographer C.S. Fly eternalized Warren when a photograph he took of the infamous prospector was used for the model of a miner for the Arizona state seal in 1912.

ZACATECAS CANYON

Zacatecas Canyon is an old thoroughfare located at the upper end of Brewery Gulch. It is a secluded neighborhood adjacent to Dubacher Canyon and below Chihuahua Hill. Another way to come into or travel out of Bisbee is on a gorgeous path currently called Ridge Line Trail.

At the turn of the twentieth century, this part of Bisbee was the neighborhood where Mexican nationals, Mexican Americans and Yaqui Indians lived. Zacatecas Canyon was a settlement developed surrounding a community dance hall and a saloon or cantina. Here, along with Chihuahua Hill, is where a series of distressing incidents took place, mostly about one hundred years ago. One incident was when an unnamed woman was killed near the end of September in Zacatecas Canyon. A drunken woodcutter was carelessly shooting his gun and accidentally hit a few sticks of dynamite with a stray bullet and blew up the hut she was living in. As time passed, more anomalies seemed to occur in the segregated neighborhood.

MEXICAN GANG IN SHOOTOUT WITH BISBEE POLICE

According to the *Bisbee Daily Review*, during the evening hours of September 3, 1922, three Bisbee police officers—Clyde Morris, William Steger and Sergeant Harry Anderson—were called to Zacatecas Canyon at 8:15 p.m. A woman called to say there was a large group of people disrupting the neighborhood and that she was frightened.

After officers visited several homes in the vicinity, they spotted a party of about fifty Hispanic men and women. The officers told the large group to quiet down. There were no negative responses from the party, so the officers started to head back to the police station. Suddenly, a man riding on horseback was coming quickly down one of the sides of the canyon. They stopped and searched him and found no justification to detain him any further. The officers began to head back to the station again. In the meantime, the crowd had dispersed and taken positions behind small houses, shacks and large boulders in the narrow canyon.

Suddenly, loud screams and shouting came from the area the officers had just left. The trio headed back when, without any kind of warning, gunfire erupted. The police officers were being shot at, and huge rocks were being thrown at them.

Officer Steger shot back; after emptying the first clip, he quickly finished another. Officer Morris's gun had jammed, and while he was trying to unjam it, he slipped on a rock and fell. Somebody directly behind Morris began to open fire on them. Steger returned fire, and when he ran out of ammunition, he and Morris ran down the canyon. As they were running, they were followed by a hail of rocks and bullets. They jumped into a car and were driven to the police station for more ammo.

Night Sergeant Anderson heard the car coming down at a high speed and met them at the police station. After gathering a big supply of ammunition, the three police officers went back to Zacatecas. They parked far enough away not to be heard and crept up the hill and easily found the gang of thugs. They were gathered near an opening of a wall that was built in a semicircle, which looked like it was used as a donkey corral. The three officers entered a gate at the opposite end of the corral, coming up behind the group. About twelve or fifteen of the men heard them and ran into the hills.

The officers separated themselves several yards apart and advanced on the seven who did not leave and told them to put their hands up. Sergeant Anderson said he was watching a Mexican national named Enrique Loya, who was standing at the end of the line of men. He suddenly picked up a rock and hurled it at Officer Morris and missed. Morris immediately saw what was happening and ordered Loya to put his hands up, instead the young man grabbed another big rock and started to throw it at Morris's head. Officer Morris fired his gun. Loya walked over to the edge of the corral and sat down. The officers did not think he was seriously wounded.

In an interview with a local newspaper, Sergeant Anderson stated, "Before we reached the gang, I told Officer Morris to watch the other six men while I and Officer Steger went into the hills to look for the others that had escaped. They couldn't find them and returned to Morris and the prisoners. During that short time, Loya appeared to be in poor shape as he was badly wounded from the gunshot after all."

The three officers got a blanket from one of the tiny houses nearby and placed it around Loya. They then took him directly to the police station and called for a doctor. Loya made it alive to the police station but died before the doctor arrived.

According to City Marshal Wertz, after reading and hearing the reports of the shooting from Morris, Sterger and Anderson, he believed the accounts matched and were true. Wertz thought Morris was thoroughly justified in shooting at the man who was attacking him. Officer Morris was exonerated by a coroner's jury in court a few days after the incident. Astonishingly enough, Morris had only been on the job a few days, as he was filling a vacancy after Officer Alva Reese had resigned. Officer Steger been with the department for only several months. He had originally worked as a police officer in San Diego, California.

Loya had a criminal record and was arrested in July of that same year by Sergeant Anderson and Officer Reese for having liquor in his possession. He was again arrested in October for a similar offense. Following his second arrest, he was turned over to immigration officers at Naco and was deported to Mexico.

The other six men were arrested and were held in the city jail until the completion of an investigation of their connection, if any, with the shooting. All the men denied any involvement with the attack on Steger and Morris. Their names were Jose Vialiobo, Jose Munoz, Alejo Madero, Ramon Robles, Sabino Corta and Felipe Lopez.

NIGHT SERGEANT SHOT IN FREAK ACCIDENT

There is always danger in doing any type of job. Bisbee police in the 1920s understood their assignment. But Lady Luck doesn't always show up, and things can always go awry. Remember the night sergeant, Harry Anderson? The same policeman who had emerged unscathed from the incident in Zacatecas Canyon? Three days later, because of a freak accident, he was shot through both of his legs!

According to an article in the *Bisbee Daily Review*, during his down time, Anderson decided to clean out a desk in City Marshal Wertz's office at city hall. The sergeant had done a little organizing in the office a few moments before and then left to go into the hallway. Officer Steger came into the office while Anderson was outside of the room.

Steger took his coat off and took the gun from his holster and laid them on the marshal's desk and left. Anderson came back into the office and grabbed the coat and, without taking notice of the pistol, hung the coat on a hook.

The six-shooter fell to the floor, hitting the front sight first, and then the hammer hit the hard ground. A bullet in the chamber fired and passed through Anderson's left calf and then his right. The bullet didn't stop there. It traveled and tore away two inches of material from the arm of the desk chair.

It was reported that Anderson ran from the police station, then to the mining company's dispensary. He was later moved to the C&A Hospital. He was out on sick leave for several weeks before he was ready to resume regular police duties.

SEVERAL ARRESTED IN LIQUOR RAID

Bisbee was not excluded from the wrath of the Prohibition years. In December 1921 in Zacatecas and Dubacher Canyons, a large amount of liquor was collected one afternoon during a raid made by Bisbee Police. They were targeting the homes of Mexicans in the area. Several men were arrested.

It was reported that three gallons of mescal were taken by Officer Reese from the house of Jesus Munoz in the Dubacher area. He was placed under arrest.

Chief Brakefield was in Zacatecas and found a keg of about ten gallons of mescal as well. That belonged to Jesus Costello.

Of course, you might speculate that with the drinking of illegal liquor, there must be some good, old-fashioned brawling. Rafael Marces and Gonzalo Leon were fined fifteen dollars each for just that. They were arrested on Chihuahua Hill, where they were so violent and vile that it was necessary to call a surgeon to tend to their wounds. The police stated that the two were both drunk.

8

BISBEE AND ITS CRITTERS

THE BISBEE BURRO

When it comes to the development of Bisbee, animals have played huge roles in its progress. Pioneers had to figure out how to get material to build their homes and to get the necessities for everyday life, including essentials such as water and fuel for cooking and heating. The beast of burden has been Bisbee's number-one pick for useful animal. They were used for delivering firewood from what was once a forest of oak trees surrounding the mining camp. Expert woodcutters from Mexico saw an opportunity to gather and load their burros and use them as a delivery service. These master woodcutters were even more in need after the mines used a great deal of material for their furnaces and for support timbers to umbrella the underground tunnels.

Burros also famously carried twenty-five-gallon canvas water bags up those same treacherous and exceptionally vertical slopes. The twenty-five-cent bags were carefully balanced on the donkeys' backs. The animals were the backbone of a beneficial enterprise with a full list of clients, not only in the residential area but also in the business district.

After some years, the donkey population in town had become exceedingly high, as they became thought of as pets more than manual workers. The hills were an excellent place for children to ride their donkeys bareback, a unique pastime. Burro owners would even pose with the animals in photo studios, holding them like anyone would pose with the family dog.

Bisbee water
mules, 1901.
*Author's
collection.*

By 1919, Chief Marshal J.A. Kempton had created the official position
of "burro catcher." He commissioned M. Jaso to round up stray or unkept
donkeys. On his first day, he managed to gather up six by noon.

An odd occurrence took place on the morning of January 19, 1902. A
donkey that was worn out from a lifetime of work stretched out on Howell
Avenue and died. Witnesses said his ears drooped and his eyes seemed to go
cold; then he collapsed. The coroner said: "Poor John. Your work is done.
You have carried your last load of wood. Your sweet thin voice will no longer
be heard at a late hour serenading the guests of the Copper Queen. You will
be missed."

WAGON MULES

In 1909, when a white mule died in Bisbee, several people believed the "hood-doo man" was to blame. The animal dropped dead, and an old superstition—that the white mule is immortal—was instantly proved untrue. It was a common belief that a white mule was one of the creatures that was passed up by the grim reaper and would last forever.

The mule, like its counterpart the burro, also hauled wood and water, but for the city. That day, the white mule was pulling a garbage wagon through town. During the morning of March 2, on Quality Hill, the mule began to stagger and stumble. When the driver unhitched it from the wagon, it instantly fell and collapsed to the ground. Moments later, it died.

The driver looked at the white mule and was completely baffled that it had succumbed to mortality. He solemnly swore that he would carry three rabbit's feet from that day forward. A local newspaper report stated that the mule was worth $250 and the city would find it difficult to locate a replacement.

In December of the same year, a commotion of trouble unfolded in the streets of Bisbee due to a very stubborn mule named Maud. The animal held up traffic at the intersection of Naco Road and Brewery Avenue at the entrance of Brewery Gulch, at the train tracks.

He was harnessed to a wagon with another mule. Maud was trained to lead but, for no apparent reason, decided to stop. The *Bisbee Review* stated that three dozen people, forty dogs, a dozen whips, three pairs of ice tongs, sixteen crowbars, four cart hooks, ten pike poles and several brooms, along with ten thousand curse words, failed to entice Maud to move. The driver was a one-legged man whose trouble started at ten in the morning. The wagon finally moved because a group of seven people were able to convince Maud to walk a short distance. They managed to get Maud all the way to the train depot until the cart was brought to a sudden stop, because Maud unexpectedly decided to sit, right in the middle of the track.

People tried everything, until Maud got up and moved about twenty yards through a large mob of howling spectators. He then made it to the Gulch and decided to lie down. People were now brushing his ribs with brooms, but it didn't work. They were near enough to Joseph Muheim's Edelweiss Café for the mule to smell the aroma of food. He made a run for the restaurant's front door when a policeman steered him in the other direction.

The cop wrestled the mule and clutched onto the harness while someone appeared with a bucketful of oats just in the nick of time. After a while, the crowd yelled, "Go on, Maud," as the mule once again refused to move. Someone whispered in Maud's ear, "Lots to drink up Brewery Gulch. Make tracks." The mule had no reaction to that. Then someone poured water in the mule's ear, while Special Officer MacDonald and Alderman Lem Shattuck showed up to join in on the "hee-haw" chorus of the crowd. Maud still didn't move an inch.

An ice wagon showed up and pushed against the mule cart. The wagon driver directed his horses forward. Maud, against his will, was forced to move to avoid being run over. Then he suddenly took off in a fast trot, and soon, he and his wagon vanished around the curve, making tracks for the upper end of the Gulch without stopping once!

In another incident, in 1904 in Lowell, where the traffic circle is now located, a sixteen-mule-team wagon and its trailer turned over. It was hauling high stacks of bags full of grain. The wagon turned too sharply around the curve in the road. Both wagon and trailer had top-heavy loads and turned over in the ditch. The driver was thrown along with the cargo. Incredibly, he wasn't hurt, and miraculously the wagon and trailer were not damaged. When the turnover happened, the mules were brought to a complete stop and stayed in the same spot without running off.

MINE MULES

Mules were also used in underground mining operations. Horses were not the animal for the job, as mules acclimate to their surroundings quickly and have a compulsion for tough work. Of course, men were the original "mules" used to push the ore carts to the surface. But with the success of a mine came the need for speed. As the demand for ore increased, so did the need for more to be hauled to the surface.

After a serious caving accident in the Holbrook shaft in 1906, mules were hoisted underground. They were to haul ore cars from that shaft to the Gardiner shaft for the long runs. It was the intention to construct an electric plant on Sacramento Hill to supply electricity on those long hauls and for all other underground operations.

During September of that same year, full-bred Missouri mules were lowered into the Copper Queen mines with a cost of approximately $200 each over a span of ten days. The company boasted that the mules were lowered without accident, with the exception of one of the animals bursting

Miners and mules underground. This is in the Brow Mine in Brown, West Virginia, in 1908. This gives a sample of what the work was like. Photos of Bisbee mining mules are rare, most likely because of lighting conditions and photography's time requirements. *Wikimedia Commons.*

a blood vessel during its struggle to break out of its harness as it was being lowered into the tunnels.

In the article "Mules at Work in the Copper Queen," it was reported that the mules would each pull a train of six ore cars. Nine years later, four mules ran out of that mine and were considered missing. A notice was put in the newspaper, "If located please communicate with the Copper Queen Consolidated Copper Company, phone 288."

The approximately one hundred Bisbee mules did astonishing work and were stabled underground. They hauled the carts weighing a total of just over three thousand pounds for about fifteen miles per day and work anywhere from two to six years. The veterinary costs and feed, along with employment of full-time blacksmiths for the mules' hooves and shoes, were well worth the money for the progress of the mine. There was another pricy expense. In an article in the *Bisbee Daily Review*, it was reported that the roofs of the tunnels had to be raised and the tunnels widened to accommodate the animals.

The miner who oversaw the mules was called a mule driver. The pay scale for that position by 1907 was four dollars a day, matching a miner's salary. The mule driver was a dedicated personality who endured much at the side of his animal. During the summer of 1910, a runaway mule was reported at the Hoatson shaft. Mule driver Albert Fassel was working through the drifts with empty ore cars. He was sitting in one of the carts when the mule pulled him along to get to the next haul. Suddenly, the mule became frightened for an unknown reason, and before Fassel could yell "whoa," they were at full speed! They were going so fast that the candle the driver was holding blew out. He was left in complete blackness and had no idea what was going to happen next.

Fortunately, the mule finally stopped on its own, because he was running upgrade, and after a while, the weight of the cars and Fassel tired him out. The mule driver, despite being thrown around the cart and hitting the mountain wall along the way, suffered only a bad scrape and a bruised right arm. Miraculously, the cars stayed on the track.

According to an announcement in the local newspaper, twenty-six-year-old mule driver Ed Johnson, while working at the Briggs shaft, broke his hip. He was trying to calm an excited mule when he slipped onto the track and a mine cart ran over him. He recovered from his injury and returned to work sometime later.

Unfortunately, some horrific things happened due to traumatic accidents involving the mules. One was the cause of a bizarre accident. In the *Bisbee Daily Review*, the article "Kick of Mule Causes Temporary Insanity" reported that miner Kit Nelson shot himself shortly after he was kicked in the back of the head by a mine mule. A coroner's jury released a verdict that the cause of Nelson's death was due to insanity.

The miner had been injured in the C&A Mine in November 1909. Remarkably, he wasn't knocked out after being kicked at the back of the head and at the base of the brain. But he was sent home. He complained of ringing in his ears with occasional deafness after the incident.

A couple of days later, after returning from downtown, he went to his bedroom while mumbling to himself about a couple of women who were after him and were going to kill him. He repeated this story to his wife several times, then asked her for his revolver. It was stated that she didn't tell him where his gun was, but he eventually found it in his trunk. The miner said he wanted to prepare in case the women, whom he claimed had called him names and threatened him on the street, should come to his room and kill him.

Mrs. Nelson said that she left the room and the next thing she heard was the gunshot and she found him lying dead on the bed. She said, "He had been acting strange ever since he was kicked by the mule, and I think that made him insane."

Kit Nelson's death certificate states that he died on November 23 at 8:00 p.m. The cause of death was a gunshot wound to his head and it was written as a suicide. He had lived in Bisbee for only five months before his death. He was from Colorado.

Gradually, the mules were retired from different mines, and on September 22, 1910, the Cole shaft was closed and the mules brought to the surface. A crowd heard about the exciting and somewhat emotional event and stood in front of the shaft. Local reporters stated that some of the animals had been in the mine for two or more years. One old fellow had spent six years underground. Witnesses said the mules displayed a great amount of happiness as soon as the sunshine hit their faces. The miners became overwhelmed with gratitude for their years of service. The retired mules were sent out to pasture at a local ranch.

The animals were the sole haulers until about 1908, when electric locomotives were introduced. The miners used both forms of towing until 1930, when the mules were replaced completely by the locomotives.

MR. BRUIN

One Bisbee pioneer was the quintessential alpha male from the turn of the twentieth century. He had a strong spirit that fed his ambitious ideas and an intelligence that gave him a genius business mind that secured him as a Bisbee heavyweight. Joseph M. Muheim Sr. came to America in 1887. The next year, he rode into Bisbee by stagecoach from Tombstone. He answered to two nicknames, "Lucky" and "Joe." He was born in Uri Göscehenen, Switzerland, on January 25, 1867, and was a nephew of the Dubacher brothers. He was also referred to as the "grubstake founder of Cananea," a mining town in Mexico.

He came to work for his uncles, who were operating a brewery in Brewery Gulch. In later years, he and other associates located several mining claims in Cananea, then sold them to Colonel William Greene for $30,000. Muheim duplicated his business transactions in the Bisbee District. He found mining claims and sold them to big mining companies for millions.

Muheim had more aspirations as he matured in the Bisbee community. So, along with his uncles and another prominent Bisbee businessman, Baptiste Caretto, he constructed some of Bisbee's most famous landmarks. This includes the Pythian Castle on OK Street, the Philadelphia Hotel, the *Bisbee*

Ore newspaper building and the "Muheim Block" in the business district of Brewery Gulch. He was involved in many committees and clubs and was one of the founders of the Miners & Merchants Bank in town.

Joseph married a woman named Carmelita in Tombstone in 1898 and moved into a house on Youngblood Hill the same year. This is now called the Muheim Heritage House Museum, located in Brewery Gulch. Joseph had the home built for his new bride, and it was completed in 1915. The couple had an ever-expanding family, and Joseph had additions made to the house to keep up with the needed space as the years went by. At the time of his death in 1951, Joseph Sr. was the last surviving original director of the Miners & Merchants Bank.

Muheim was clever and seemed to grasp the concept of marketing to make money. This includes a very bizarre story regarding the infamous brewery where he bartended and where Brewery Gulch derived its name. This charismatic person was popular with local miners and was given a black bear cub as a gift. A miner who had found the animal in the Huachuca Mountains decided that Muheim would be happy to receive such a present and would make a great owner of the wild animal.

Joe accepted the black bear as a saloon pet and kept "Mr. Bruin" throughout its life. Over the years, the bear became acclimated to saloon life and was pampered and spoiled with attention from Muheim and patrons. He became well known to the customers who came in daily, and they became quite attached to the animal. Mr. Bruin even learned how to box with miners and cowboys.

According to an article written by Bill Epler, "Gulch Bear Loved Beer & Miners," in the book *Bisbee Vignettes*, the cub became very popular and was given beer by the brewery patrons on a regular basis. Eventually, Mr. Bruin was able to chug a quart of beer as quickly as the hardy Bisbee miners. When he became a little tipsy, he would begin rough horseplay with patrons.

Mr. Bruin took part in regular friendly boxing matches. The bear and the miners took turns pushing one another. The contest was to see who could push—or, rather, slap—the farthest, man or bear. Epler wrote that a miner would land a hard one on the bear, making him slide over a little, but then the animal would pound his opponent with the pads of his paw, slamming the man the full length of the bar and knocking him to the ground! Not surprisingly, the miner would get back up and go toe-to-toe with Mr. Bruin.

The Muheim bear grew to stand on his two hind legs to a height of about six feet, and he weighed three hundred pounds. As he grew larger, Muheim Sr. became nervous about the safety of his patrons. Even though his bear was

Joseph Muheim and the notorious "Mr. Bruin" in front of his brewery. *Author's collection.*

always forgiving after each boxing match and was happy to receive beer in payment, Muheim grew anxious and worried that a random miner would be mangled or even killed. So he made the decision to have the bear destroyed. Because Mr. Bruin was so loved by the miners, cowboys and Bisbee residents, Muheim couldn't find anyone to take the job as hitman.

One afternoon, a little girl about the age of five came into the saloon with her father. She had a bag of candy in her hand. This caught the complete attention of Mr. Bruin, who was relaxing on the floor. The bear went directly to the child to sniff the bag. She immediately put the candy behind her back, but Mr. Bruin put the child in a bear hug, literally, trying to reach for the sweets.

Joseph jumped over from behind the bar and hit the bag of candy out of the girl's hand and scattered the candy all over the floor. The bear promptly left the child alone and went to the sprawled-out sweets. At that moment, Joe decided to destroy the animal, regardless of anybody's opinion.

Sometimes, things have a way of working itself out. Each night when the saloon was closed, the Muheim bear was chained to a large cottonwood

The Muheim Block today and the site of the Bisbee pioneer's The Brewery Saloon. *Author's collection.*

tree near the building. An iron ring was put around the tree's trunk and a chain was put around the animal's neck. Ironically, on the night of the candy incident, Mr. Bruin was as drunk as a bear could be and was ready to sleep. It was reported that when Mr. Bruin was secured with the chain, he climbed the tree trunk to a favorite large branch and positioned himself for the night, then went directly to sleep.

At sunrise, an unnamed bartender ran to Muheim's home and shook him from his sleep. He said: "Joe! Joe! Who's strung up in the cottonwood tree behind the Brewery?"

Muheim ran directly to the saloon and stopped in his tracks as his eyes caught sight of Mr. Bruin swinging from the chain around his neck. It was the bear and not a person who was hanging from the tree. He had evidently been more inebriated than anyone suspected. Tragically, sometime during the night, he slipped through the tree's branches and hanged himself.

FELIX THE MINE CAT

Early miners from days when tunnels were dug out by hand had an ancient conundrum that had an easy fix. Mine rats were a curse and at certain times a blessing. A rat would signal an approaching cave-in by running away and giving time for men to escape to safety. One extraordinary feline was a cat named Felix, who worked the Bisbee Sacramento Division 7 shaft.

In a *Bisbee Daily Review* article from 1912, W.B. Gohring, superintendent for the Calumet and Arizona Mining Company, asked a reporter if they had heard of the company's cats. Gohring stated that they had house cats underground. After some time, they became slightly wild, stronger and more productive. He said, "They're fine ratters too, and before long we will have them in all our mines."

In the fall of 1912, the mining companies in town were having trouble with rats, which would eat the timbers out and do other serious damage in the tunnels. They set different types of traps and poisons, but those never worked. They finally decided on cats as an aid to their situation. Gohring said: "Tom and Tabby are quickly cleaning up our mines. Just as soon as we can get enough cats to go around, we are going to place them in all our mines."

At that time, the Copper Queen Consolidated Mining Company was also putting cats in the mines. They hired a person who oversaw their feeding. A local dairy man would deliver several gallons of milk for the cats daily. The cat attendant was to keep the felines content.

Bisbee merchants complained that they had a great number of rats in their stores, damaging their merchandise. They claimed that the rodents were from the mines, and they agreed that anything that included the extermination of the rats was something they approved of.

In the *Copper Queen Bulletin* of May 1927, the article "FELIX Fifteen Years Continuous Service" states that the cat was born underground at the Sacramento Division 7 in 1912. This shaft had three compartments and was eventually used as a main hoisting shaft. Felix's patrol duties were at the 1,500-foot level.

Miners loved this cat and said he was an outstanding employee and never missed a shift. The black cat was quite comfortable during the many years he lived in the tunnels and would follow the mining train tracks as he traveled. Although living as a contented cat, he was shy. He was known to be affectionate to only a few miners, but in his golden years he became more responsive and affectionate toward others.

He probably wasn't paying attention one day when he laid his tail near the wheel of a train car and the unthinkable happened. Without Felix noticing the train beginning to move, his tail was crushed! A powderman saw the poor cat and quickly took action. He took an axe and freed Felix from the train car. The miner amputated part of Felix's tail in such a way that it left a sharply angled tip, which became his trademark.

When the mining cat died on June 15, 1927, the mining company bragged that he had caught 5,292 rats in his lifetime—a feat any cat would be proud of. An article from the July issue of the *Copper Queen Bulletin* says he was buried in a wooden dynamite box with all honors on the surface at the Sacramento shaft. This was Felix's first and last trip to the surface, as in his lifetime he was never able to bathe in the sunshine or purr in its warm delight.

THE BISBEE FLY-SWATTING CONTEST OF 1912

Bisbee had a rough start regarding the booming city's sanitary conditions, until it became an incorporated city in 1902. The residents contended with typhoid fever, smallpox and other illnesses and diseases. Even though the town sits a mile high in the mountains, it still is in the desert, and before the streets were paved, they were made of dirt. The dust clung to everything, including inside houses, and during monsoon season, the streets were turned into marshes. A crisis arose for the citizens from 1888 to 1890: the drinking water was taken from shallow wells, causing a typhoid epidemic, which sadly took the lives of hundreds of people in just those two years.

About twenty-two years later, sanitation was better, but the health department held an interesting event to control the breeding of the common housefly. The *Bisbee Daily Review* published a series of articles reporting on the situation and the new ideas the local governments had in mind. With the Commercial Club of Bisbee, a health campaign was conducted during the spring months called "Swat that fly or it may get you." This genius of an idea led to approximately one million flies being killed annually.

Across the country, similar fly-killing campaigns were held, but the county health officer and city health officer, along with Secretary J.H. Gray of the Warren District Commercial Club, made an announcement for a competition more serious than the kind previous held. The contest would begin in August 1912. The slogan for this contest was, "Swat the fly and get a prize."

The reasoning for the newly formed competition was that, just over a week before the announcement, there was a fly infestation in every area of Bisbee. No one could figure out where the flies came from, but there were tens of thousands of pests thriving in the humidity at that time of year. The environment was a perfect haven for breeding, and people were seeing more and more of them every day.

The Commercial Club offered a prize of $10.00 to the individual adult or child who killed the most flies in the month of August and through the first part of September. Second prize was $7.50; third prize was $5.00; and fourth prize was $2.50. The county health officer would be the judge of the contest and would be responsible to count or measure the flies killed. The accepted standard of measurement was 1,600 dry flies to a gill. This is a unit of volume usually used for liquids. A gill is defined as half a cup or four fluid ounces.

Quotes form the several different articles included, "A fly killed in time kills nine others," "Early to bed and early to rise, get a swatter and kill the flies," and, maybe most important, "An ounce of prevention by killing flies is worth a pound of typhoid cure."

There were really no strict rules, as it didn't matter how a fly was killed. The main objective was to "swat the fly." There was one exception: wet flies were not accepted. The government officials encouraged everyone in every part of Bisbee, including satellite communities such as Lowell and Warren, to get their cash prize. Packages of dead flies could be delivered to the Commercial Club office or at the Ball and Bledsoe Drug Store. The deadline was 6:00 p.m. on September 3, but committee members would be counting throughout the competition.

Toward the end of the contest, people were reporting that there was a big drop in the number of flies and were pleased to think that the typhoid carriers were now incapable of passing the disease on to loved ones. Many flies were thought to have died naturally, but more were killed, and this prevented millions of others from hatching.

By August 9, the newspaper was already reporting some updates. The numbers of dead flies ranged from 5,200 to 89,600. More than 250,000 flies were counted and were being credited to the children living in the Warren District. At that rate, the expected number was to be above 2,750,000; again, 1,600 was the approximate count for each gill of flies turned in.

Some advice was given on how to kill the flies. One was to make homemade traps and place them in stores or homes. A trap could be made from wire mosquito netting, formed in a cone shape with a funnel at the top for an entrance and tacked down to a piece of wood for a base. In the trap one could place a saucer of sweetened water to attract the flies. Another idea was to place a saucer containing formaldehyde and water and a large piece of bread. The formaldehyde would kill the pests, but conveniently, they would most likely fall to their deaths, surrounding the trap. Dr. Miner from the county joyously stated that it gave him great pleasure to see 338,000 flies go up in smoke. He burned them as soon as they were counted.

Finally, the contest was completed; over two million flies were killed. This was an incredible achievement, as the *Bisbee Daily Review* reported that each fly could carry more than one thousand germs. With the announcement of the winner, the fly committee made sure to give the youth of the community credit for the lower number of typhoid fever cases originating in Bisbee that season compared with the number from the previous year and many years before the contest.

The winner of the Bisbee fly contest of 1912 was a young boy named Richard Philips, with a total of 493,200 flies killed. One girl, Rilla Wacek, made the top ten. She took sixth place with 92,600 flies killed. Sadly, two contestants had included wet files in their entries, and those were never counted.

9

APACHES AND
THE INDIAN DRILLS

THE INDIAN SCOUT

Indian scouts worked for the U.S. Army during many wars and were trained in reconnaissance, but it is for the Indian Wars (1849–86) that they may be most recognized. Traditionally, these men looked out for their clan in order to protect them from enemies and to hunt for game and seek new places to camp. They came from several tribes, but the Chiricahua Apache scout stands out. General George Crook had great admiration for these scouts. He said that Chiricahuas were the most subordinate, energetic, untiring and, by odds, the most efficient of his command.

According to an article by Jessie Kratz in the *National Archives*, the Apache Campaign of the American Indian Wars was fought between the 1870s and 1886. Several other conflicts where unfolding within a grander military campaign to control westward expansion directly after the Mexican-American War. During these conflicts, Geronimo led a group of his men in resistance to the federal interests and for the welfare of his people, who were being resettled on reservations. The great warrior was captured in 1877 and put on the San Carlos Reservation. By 1881, Geronimo had left San Carlos with many of his men, who all went to Mexico to escape. He was caught in 1884 and forced to return to the reservation but decided to leave the next year.

General George Cook had captured Geronimo once but was never able to capture him again. Brigadier General Nelson Miles replaced Cook by 1886.

Incredible documentation of Apache scouts and soldiers on Castle Rock. *Opie Burgess Collection, courtesy Bisbee Mining & Historical Museum.*

Apache scouts pose gallantly for the camera, circa late 1880s. *Author's collection.*

Miles appointed Lieutenant Charles Gatewood to capture the Apache, as Gatewood had a deeper knowledge of the Apache people. The lieutenant hired two Chiricahua Apache Indian scouts to find and give Geronimo the message that he and his band of men should surrender. They were an immense help to Miles, Gatewood and the Sixth Cavalry to get the great warrior to do just that on September 4, 1886. The Apache Indian scout helped advance the power and control to such an extent that the conflicts ended earlier than predicted.

Bisbee was discovered under the umbrella of a scout coming to the area looking for rebel Chiricahua Apaches, who were thought to have an encampment there.

The Stagecoach Ran Hard and Fast

In the late 1800s, the passenger train nearest Bisbee was at Contention, Arizona. Just to get to Tombstone from the train station, you had to ride the stagecoach. Then, if you were traveling to the mining camp called Bisbee, you had to do the same. The driver of the Modoc Stagecoach would run the horses hard and fast, because he and the passengers were fearful of Apaches or members of the Cochise County Cowboys attacking them on the way. An armed Wells Fargo agent rode along, acting as a guard to protect the passengers and anything of value on board.

The stagecoach was small, uncomfortable and blanketed with dust during its journeys. As the stagecoach traveled quickly, the driver would call to his horses with a voice that was deep and loud while cracking his whip to keep his horse team at a quick pace. The ride was rough, as it went over large rocks, through deep washes and thick bushes, also dodging an assortment of desert wildlife on its way. The trip to the mining town would be a ride lasting for hours on a rugged path with lots of jolting and dust spraying in the passengers' eyes and mouths. Along the ride, the passengers were said to be filled with a trembling fear of the Apaches, who could see the stagecoach from the Cochise Stronghold in the far distance. Several reports continuously alerted the stagecoach that there were sightings of Apaches near Bisbee and Tombstone.

The adrenaline-filled ride to Bisbee sometimes ended with even more excitement. The stagecoach had to climb the narrow and treacherous road, now called the North Old Divide Road. The coach would stop at Banning's Toll Gate to pay a ten-cent tax on every person, horse, driver and luggage. This is where the six-horse team would be watered and changed out, if needed, to pull the stagecoach to its destination of Bisbee, which was on the other side of the mountain. Often, the driver would have to pull aside as soon as he found room to let an ore wagon through. Coming from behind, the passengers would hear the twenty-four-mule team pulling a large amount of weight, making a thunderous sound of hooves, wagon wheels and jangling from the iron chains and harnesses. Along with those boisterous sounds, one would also hear the tremendous voice of the mule skinner directing his mule team, which added to the thrilling experience.

BISBEE AND THE INDIAN SCARES

During the early 1880s, Bisbee had its own chapter in the history books with problematic situations with the Chiricahua Apaches. Before the town was established and when the area was thick with bushes and wildlife, the war chief of the Apache tribe, Geronimo, visited often. When the leader and his men were traveling through this area, the clean, cool springs of the future mining camp was a meeting place for them. When prospectors and miners came in with families, the Apaches weren't pleased, believing the area was their territory. In this situation, the residents of the Bisbee mining camp were in constant fear of an "Indian attack." The location was not going to be given up without some sort of conflict between the Chiricahua Apaches and those who were intent on making a living there.

According to several historical reports, Geronimo had camped there often. There used to be a spring where the Muheim Block now stands. This is where he stayed. Between 1877 and 1886, the residents of the mining camp lived in an anxious state and in constant turmoil over the fear of the band of Apaches conducting any type of aggression against them.

In 1974, Cora Thorp wrote in the *Cochise County Quarterly* about Bisbee's "Indian Raids," which left an impression of the fear that parents, teachers and the community must have felt in 1881. Thorp wrote that one of the first lessons a student would learn in the Bisbee one-room schoolhouse was what to do during an Indian drill. The established code was four blasts—two short and one long and then one short again—from the work whistle at the Copper Queen Mine. When that signal was heard, an Apache was sighted.

The Glory Hole tunnel, with miners standing on a deck. This is where the legendary shelter for woman and children was located. *Author's Collection.*

The children were to form in groups of four and hold hands and follow the teacher, Clara J. Stillman. She was Bisbee's first teacher. They were not to leave the school until a second signal was blown. Only then were the students led to the designated shelter, where they were then told to run to the Copper Queen Mine, later called the Glory Hole Tunnel. The assigned location was always supplied with food and water.

Thorp wrote that on the fortieth anniversary of Bisbee, Stillman gave a speech about her experiences teaching in the first little schoolhouse, located at Castle Rock. She said that one day, the mine whistle blew its signal and she and her students ran down the canyon as fast as they could and made it to the Glory Hole Tunnel. There, they joined the women of the camp. One of the ladies was holding on tight to her apron with what Stillman thought were valuable items. The woman said out loud, "At least I saved my silver!" Then she let her apron skirt fall, and silver items didn't roll out. It was her weekly mending of stockings and socks that hit the dirt floor instead. It was a nice distraction from the fear that was overwhelming everyone in that shelter.

William Daniels Killed by Apaches

The fear of the Apaches attacking Bisbee stayed with its residents until Geronimo was finally captured in the fall of 1886. He never did attack the mining camp, but a tragic event took place during the summer before that raised anxiety to its highest. It was the killing of a man named William "Billy" Daniels by Apaches in 1885. Daniels was well known throughout the Arizona Territory and was somehow connected with the Cochise County sheriff's office. He was said to come from the far eastern United States and came to the West to "kill an Indian."

Several articles in local newspapers have detailed the event and reported that about four miles outside of Bisbee was a place called Forrest Ranch. The *Tombstone* published an article, "An Eyewitness of the Death of W.A. Daniels," under the column titled Indian News. Milton Gilman was interviewed and had a firsthand account.

Gilman stated that he and Daniels went to Forrest Ranch to try to gather horses for a posse to track the Apache group that had been spotted the day before. Witnesses reported seeing signal fires in Dixie Canyon and that Apaches had circled around the low hills of Tombstone, heading east through the Dragoon Mountains. This specific area was known to the Apaches as the "abode of the dead." The Apaches believed this is where the spirits of their deceased ancestors would speak softly in sighs and moans, through the evening wind. This is where they were last spotted and seen heading to Forrest Ranch.

There were no horses available for Gilman and Daniels, as the livestock were out on the range. The ranch owner had his fourteen-year-old son look for the horses. Meanwhile, Gillam and Daniels began to track and look for any new clues as to where the Apache men were. They ended up with horses to ride and rode about ten miles, when they were shocked to find approximately fifty different sets of fresh tracks. Daniels was positive the Apaches were heading to Dixie Canyon, so they started to head in that direction on their horses.

Gilman looked up toward a canyon and saw a large amount of Apache men and the smoke of their camp fires. He showed Daniels who then looked through his binoculars. He told Gilman there were a thousand of them up there. He then said they needed to get out of there. They took off in a fast run but were cut off by seven or eight Apaches they hadn't seen before.

Daniels fired two shots at them with his revolver, and Gilman took four shots with his Winchester while running in the other direction. They rode

Chihuahua Hill proudly overlooks the old mining town, now a haven for artists. *Author's collection.*

side-by-side as the Apache men were on their tail. Suddenly, Daniels was shot in the leg; the ball from one of the Apache's guns went clear through and then hit the horse. Daniels's horse leaped into the air, then fell, breaking its neck. Daniels was thrown off. At that moment, the young Forrest teen rode up to them and emptied his rifle, hitting no one. Ignoring the young man's gunshots, as soon as Daniels hit the ground an Apache man went up to him and shot him seven times in the head, then smashed his jawbone with the butt of his gun. Then the rest of the Apache group took the dead man's coat, vest, saddle and bridle from his dead horse.

Gilman and the boy rode as fast as their horses could carry them down the road when they met up with three teamsters with wagons hauling lumber to Bisbee along with three horsemen who were also from there and were coming over the hill. The Apaches saw the wagon and men on the road and turned around and took off in the opposite direction. At this point, everyone helped to retrieve Daniels's body and took it to the Forrest house and then to Bisbee.

The *Tombstone* reported that soon after, ranchers in the vicinity rounded up their horses, driving them out to Ochoaville. The reporter wrote, "They have taken all their men and their families into the same place for safety. They say that the San Jose and Mule Mountains are full of Indians."

BIBLIOGRAPHY

Arizona Historical Society. 1844–1890 Papers, 1888–1907. "MS 730 Sieber, Albert."

Arizona Rangers. Accessed 2023. http://www.azrangers.us.

Arizona Republic. "Spouse Slays Wife, Two Men, Self in Bisbee." April 2, 1940.

Arizona Republican. "Bisbee Quiet after Negro Troops Riot." July 5, 1919.

———. "Tenth Cavalry Troops Engage Bisbee Police." July 4, 1919.

Arizona Silver Belt (Globe, AZ). "Global Sights and Silver Beltlets." October 8, 1906.

———. "Lee Claims Self Defense." November 11, 1906.

Arizona State Board of Health. "Death Certificate Charles S. Cloud." April 1, 1940.

Bisbee (AZ) Daily Review. "Adobe Building John Smith Remembers Erection of Old Landmark on Main Street." March 18, 1908.

———. "All Women and Children Keep off Street Today." July 12, 1917.

———. "Atempt Suicide by Caller." December 9, 1908.

———. "Bankeeper Takes Poison And Ends All." March 18, 1908.

———. "Bisbee Man Will Attempt Leap of Death." April 7, 1909.

———. "Carpenter Slays Self by Shooting." June 19, 1909.

———. "C.C. Warner Killed in Shaft at Holbrook Mine." June 14, 1904.

———. "City Local and Social News." January 19, 1909.

———. "City News." October 20, 1908.

———. "Complete Resume of Labor Disturbances in State for Month." July 22, 1917.

———. "Copper Queen to Add Big Store." Feburary 28, 1906.

———. "Cororner's Jury Recommends Mercy." December 8, 1907.

———. "County and Territorial News." October 28, 1909.

———. "Death of Wife Leads White Try Kill Self." November 1, 1912.

———. "Decision to Be Rendered Tomorrow." November 16, 1913.

———. "Deported by Deputy Sheriffs." July 13, 1917.

———. "Deported from District by Citizens." July 13, 1917.

———. "Deported Men Army Guests at Columbus." July 14, 1917.

———. "Deputy Faces Charges of Assult." October 7, 1919.

———. "Deputy's Hearing Changed to October 17." October 11, 1919.

———. "Discoverer George Warren First Locator in District." August 6, 1905.

———. "Five Wounded in Streets of Bisbee as Police and Negroes Exchange Shots." July 4, 1919.

———. "Frightful Wreck." March 6, 1902.

———. "Government Orders 1200 I.W.W. TAKEN TO COLUMBUS." July 14, 1917.

———. "Haigler Jury Out Twenty Minutes." April 28, 1914.

———. "Haigler to Be Released." March 29, 1914.

———. "Hate and Disorder in the Tenderloin." May 7, 1911.

———. "Horrible Accident on the P&D." Feburary 14, 1904.

———. "Hot Air Was Too Strong for Finely." April 16, 1909.

———. "Husband Kills Rival with Gun." November 7, 1906.

———. "Jury Acquits Otto Laine in Six Minutes." November 11, 1919.

———. "Killed Her Husband." August 4, 1905.

———. "Lee Released from Charge of Murder." December 10, 1907.

———. "Lee Woman Involved in Murder." May 24.

———. "Left Hand Blown Off." November 19, 1904.

———. "Life Lost in Spray Mine." February 2, 1906.

———. "Local Personal Section." December 23, 1913.

———. "Lowell Deputy Bound over to Higher Court." October 18, 1919.

———. "Lowell Deputy Sheriff Shoots Prisoner Down in Cold Blood." October 5, 1919.

———. "M'Bride Not Guilty, Says the Jury." December 8, 1907.

———. "Mexican Quarters Raided Yesterday; Several Arrested." December 28, 1921.

———. "Mrs. Kate Savage Acquited." October 18, 1906.

———. "Mrs. Savage in Jail." August 5, 1905.

———. "Mules at Work in Copper Queen." September 2, 1906.

———. "Murder of M'Rae Lamented In the City & District." July 13, 1917.

———. "Negroes Will Perhaps Have Own School." March 2, 1910.

———. "News Notes." May 10, 1919.

———. "Not Dead, But Sleeping Chas. Warner Is Buried." June 14, 1904.

———. "Notice Section—Case Dismissed." Feburary 19, 1904.

———. "108,800 Dead Flies Wait Owner; Halts Prize Award." September 6, 1912.

———. "One Third Million Flies Swatted; War Continues." September 9, 1912.

———. "Pelican Is Killed in San Pedro Valley." May 10, 1904.

———. "Police Ambushed by Mexicans." September 5, 1922

———. "Puss Is Busy in the Mines." November 23, 1912.

———. "Rail Road Man Is Shot Down." February 22, 1920.

———. "Refugee Stockade to Be Utlized For Wobblies." July 14, 1917.

———. "Rinehart Goes East to Buy Drug Stock." May 2, 1906.

———. "Scott Gets Out of Tight Place." January 4, 1904.

———. "Sensation at Close." August 9, 1905.

———. "Sergeant Harry Anderson Shot Thru Both Legs." September 6, 1922.

———. "Stories of the Early Days of Cochise County." November 26, 1911.

———. "Stranger Makes Bold Stand for His Over in St. Elmo on Grafters." August 16, 1903.

———. "Swat Contest closes at 6 p.m. on Tuesday." August 1912.

———. "Swat the Fly Cop a Prize Champ for Month Gets $10." April 4, 1912.

———. "Takes Life with Gun." Feburary 26, 1913.

———. "The Town in Brief." March 4, 1908.

———. "Three Shots at Scott." January 2, 1903.

———. "Tips of Town Funeral of Nat Anderson." February 25, 1920.

———. "Two Killed Instantly, 1 Wounded in Crowded Cafe by Bisbee Shooter." November 9, 1913.

———. "Would Marry French Girl to Save Her." July 12, 1908.

Burgress, Opie Rundle. *Bisbee Not so Long Ago.* San Antonio, TX: Naylor Company, 1967.

Chisholm, Joe. 1949. *Brewery Gulch: Frontier Days of the Great Southwest.* San Antonio, TX: Naylor Company.

Cochise Quarterly 4, nos. 2 and 3 (June and September 1974).

Cochise Review (Bisbee, AZ). "Another Killing." Jaunary 29, 1901.

———. "Editorial News." January 5, 1901.

———. "New Code of Laws." December 29, 1900.

———. "The United Globe." March 2, 1901.

Copper Era (Clifton, AZ). "Haigler's Bond." November 9, 1914.

Copper Queen Bulletin (Bisbee, AZ). "Felix Breaks Fifteen Year Service Record When Overtaken by Grim Reaper." July 1927.

———. "Felix Fifteen Years Continous Service." May 1912.

Corbett, Peter. "Mule Pass Tunnel Has Eased Trip to-from Bisbee for 60 Years." *ADOT Communications* (blog). Arizona Department of Transportation. Arizona Highways. April 11, 2018. Accessed 2022. http:arizonahighways.com.

Cox, Annie M. "History of Bisbee 1877 to 1937." Master's thesis, University of Arizona, Tucson, 1938.

Daily Arizona Silver Belt (Globe, AZ). "Leaves House while Burning." May 24, 1907.

Death Certificate Howard Trehern. April 1, 1940.

Death Certificate Iter Trehern. April 1, 1940.

Death Certificate Roy Sanders. April 1, 1940.

Dysktra, Robert. *The Cattle Towns*. New York: Alfred Knopf, 1968.

Eakin, Britain. "Drinking It All In." Tucsonweekly.com, July 12, 2012.

Fort Worth Daily Gazette. "A Day at Dallas." February 24, 1884.

Green, Dr. Catlin. *Dr. Catlin R. Green History-Archaelogy-Lectures & Seminars.* January 22, 2022. Accessed 2023. http://www.catlingreen.org.

Kratz, Jessie. "A Real Injustice Was Done to These Two Old Scouts: The VA Claim of an Indian Scout." National Archives, 2017.

Maklary, Fran. *Mi Reina: Don't Be Afraid*. Baltimore, MD: Publish America, 2004.

Michno, Gregory. 2003. *Encyclopedia of Indian Wars: Western Battles and Skirmishes, 1850–1890*. Missoula, MT: Mountain Press Publishing.

Museum, Bob Newman-Courtesy The Bisbee Mining & Historical. n.d. "Clara Allen and Her Club 41 Best Known of Bisbee Dens."

Museum, Document from Bisbee Mining & Historical. n.d. "Vertical File." *Bisbee Women "Prostitutes."*

Palace Saloon Restaurant & Saloon. Accessed 2023. https://whiskeyrowpalace.com.

Powers, Francine. 2020. *Haunted Bisbee*. Charleston, SC: The History Press.

———. *Haunted Cochise County*. Charleston, SC: The History Press, 2023.

Prescott (AZ) Daily. "Bisbee Husband Killed by Wife." August 16, 1905.

Stokes, Richard. "Bisbee No Good for Chinaman." *Cochise Quarterly* 3, no. 4 (December 1973).

Tombstone (AZ). "An Eyewitness of the Death of W.A. Daniels." June 11, 1885.

Tombstone (AZ) Epitaph. "Doings in the Superior Court." May 3, 1914.

———. "Find No Clues to Killing Nat Anderson." April 29, 1920.

Tombstone (AZ) Nugget. "A Desperate Street Fight." October 1881.

Tucson (AZ) Daily Citizen. "Three Killed by Bisbee Man." April 2, 1940.

United States Coast Guard U.S. Department of Homeland Security. Accessed 2023. http://www.history.USCG.mil.

Weekly Champion. "Local Matters." September 19, 1985.

ABOUT THE AUTHOR

FRANCINE POWERS is an Arizona Newspaper Foundation award-winning reporter and a member of the Cochise County Historical Society. She has been featured in numerous newspaper and magazine articles, made an appearance on the television program *Ghost Hunters* and has been spotlighted on many podcasts and radio shows. She was the owner of Bisbee Haunted Historical Tours from 2013 to 2016. Additionally, she was the editor-in-chief of her own online paranormal magazine, *Spirits of Cochise County*. She is a Bisbee native and author of *Mi Reina: Don't Be Afraid* (2004), the first ghost book of its kind in Bisbee. She is also the author of *Haunted Bisbee*, which was adapted into a children's book *Ghostly Tales of Bisbee*, and *Haunted Cochise County*.

Visit us at
www.historypress.com